the rosary

the
rosary

a path into prayer

LIZ KELLY

LOYOLAPRESS.

CHICAGO

LOYOLAPRESS.

3441 N. ASHLAND AVENUE
CHICAGO, ILLINOIS 60657
(800) 621-1008
WWW.LOYOLABOOKS.ORG

The Scripture quotations contained herein are from the New Revised Standard Version Bible: Catholic Edition copyright © 1993 and 1989 by the Division of Christian Education of the National Council of the Churches of Christ in the U.S.A. Used by permission. All rights reserved.

English translation of the Apostles' Creed, the Lord's Prayer, the Hail Mary, and the Doxology by the International Consultation on English Texts.

Poem #12 (entire) from *Selected Poems of Rainer Maria Rilke,*edited and translated by Robert Bly. Copyright © 1981 by Robert Bly. Reprinted by permission of HarperCollins Publishers, Inc.

Excerpt from *The Seven Storey Mountain* by Thomas Merton, copyright 1948 by Harcourt, Inc. and renewed 1976 by the Trustees of The Merton Legacy Trust, reprinted by permission of the publisher.

Excerpt from *Feminine Spirituality: Reflections on the Mysteries of the Rosary* by Rosemary Haughton, copyright 1976 by Paulist Press. Reprinted by permission of the publisher.

Cover and interior design by Erin VanWerden
Author photo by Dave Hawkins

Library of Congress Cataloging-in-Publication Data
Kelly, Liz, 1967–
 The rosary : a path into prayer / Liz Kelly.
   p. cm.
 ISBN 0-8294-2024-X
  1. Rosary. I. Title.
BX2163.K39 2004
242'.74—dc22

                                        2004002585

Printed in the United States of America
40 05 06 07 08 09 10 Bang 10 9 8 7 6 5 4 3 2 1

For both my mothers, Mary.

Contents

Acknowledgments

My sincere thanks to all the following for sharing your expertise, encouragement, and good humor.

Jim Manney, Joe Durepos, Vinita Wright, Mike Aquilina, Charlie Flood, Dan and June McCorison, Laura Treese, Julianne Vickers, the Bridge Fellowship, Edgar and Lauri Struble, Steve McDonnell, Melanie Adams, Sr. Annamaria Stadick and the Sisters of the Schoenstatt order, and Fr. Jim Armour. Special thanks to Mark Hall and Sisters Terese and Marian of Aquinas College in Nashville for directing my attentions in your library.

To my dearest friend in prayer, Pamela, faithful over so many miles and seasons and circumstances, where would I be without your constancy and love? You wear Christ so beautifully, my friend. Thank you for helping to soften my heart before our tender heavenly Father.

My deep and lasting gratitude goes to all who've "held the lamp" for me in dark places, especially Robert and Cristia. I love you.

And to my mother and father, thank you for "inscribing" your own devotion on my writing desk and on my life.

Why the Rosary?

"Why are two billion Hail Marys said daily?"
—*Life,* December 1996

Why the Rosary?

When children ask questions about the universe, such as "Why is the sky blue?" it's likely that they are not looking for scientifically precise answers. Their burgeoning curiosity probably has more to do with their driving need for connection—to their parents and to the world—than with their desire to clearly understand the physical principles of nature. Still, as their brains begin to discover the laws of cause and effect, they are anxious to make their own connections, to find their own place in relationship to things.

When you or someone else asks, "Why the rosary?" the real question probably goes much deeper than mere theology or church tradition. You may really be asking, "What does the rosary have to do with my life?" or "Will the rosary really help me?" Or you may be saying, "Please translate all the odd legends and practices into something that has meaning to me." "Why the rosary?" is a question asked by people who are searching for connection, for meaning, even for help.

It's a legitimate question. If you have doubts about rosary meditation, you are not alone. For all of the two billion Hail Marys that are said daily, an equal number of questions are likely raised about it. Why then, when there are so many other methods by which one might meditate, would someone pick up rosary beads?

First, let's go through some of the objections. Do any of these sound familiar?

Some people feel that praying the rosary is a pious practice from the distant past that has little relevance for them today. "The rosary is outdated. It's boring. It's for little old ladies and children. It's repetitive and nonsensical. It does not fit with my active lifestyle."

Others object on very different grounds: they feel that the rosary is a highly demanding devotion only suitable for prayer "specialists." "I'm not a monk, priest, deacon, or sister. I'm too young. I'm not holy enough. I'm not highly educated. I don't have enough time, imagination, energy, willpower, self-discipline to say the rosary effectively."

Then there are those who believe that the rosary does not fit into what they think is a modern lifestyle. "I'm too hip, too together, too liberated, too intelligent, too sophisticated to be praying this way."

Many are disturbed by what they think are the ominous implications of a habit of rosary devotion. "If I say the rosary, I'll have to become a nun, priest, deacon, monk, religious nut. What will people think?"

In short, it's not uncommon for those unfamiliar with rosary devotion to respond with hesitation, indifference, fear, disbelief, cynicism, antagonism, laughter, mockery, even outright disdain. I believe these objections are based primarily on common misconceptions. The rosary is a practical and gratifying means of meditation suitable for everyone. It is simple but profound, both traditional and modern. It is easy to say the rosary, but the spiritual riches of this devotion are as deep and spiritually satisfying as any prayer discipline you can practice.

The variety of people who practice rosary devotion might come as a surprise.

Kate, a songwriter who is not even a Catholic, said, "It gives me a sense of comfort."

Kenneth, a nurse who works a very demanding schedule, said, "I feel closer to God when I pray the rosary. I feel at peace. It helps me to get through my workday."

Charles, a college student and an ex-convict, said he prays the rosary because "it is so powerful! It helped to change me."

Jennifer, a new mother, said after praying the rosary for some time, "I've found myself really turned away from and turned-off by materialism. [The rosary] seems to have opened my eyes to an entirely new world: one where spiritual matters are so much more important and more interesting than physical things."

Rudolph, a Dominican priest, commented that "when I pray the rosary regularly, I worry far less and am more at peace with the world in general."

Margaret, a lifelong devotee at eighty years old, said, "It's like a conversation with the Blessed Mother, and you know nothing helps you better than to have someone to talk to about your problems."

Perhaps the most common problem people have with the rosary is their bewilderment that something so simple—a repetitious fingering of a string of beads while praying—can yield such great spiritual benefits. They think, "How can something like this bring me closer to God?"

The rosary is not magic. It's not going to rob you of your personality or turn you into a religious fanatic. It's not a superstitious ritual or the mechanical rattling off of antiquated prayers that have little depth or meaning. The myriad people who practice this devotion have found it to be a powerful prayer, a tool of transformation, and a traditional meditation that is well suited even to this modern world.

How well suited? Many have found that the rosary has been an effective prayer to help them overcome a character defect. Joe, an attorney in a high-profile law firm, said that the things that used to set off his temper and send his blood pressure soaring now don't seem so bothersome. "I've realized I'm not alone here, trying to do everything by myself," he said. Others have found themselves freed of addictions, crippling self-pity, or nagging resentments.

Still others have found that the rosary has been effective in intercession. Rod, a thirty-two-year-old writer, prayed many rosary novenas for the intention that he would meet a woman and marry or, if that wasn't God's will, that he would be able to accept and be content with single life. In time he did marry; he and his wife just had their first child. A grandmother concerned about the religious education of her grandchildren prayed the rosary, asking that her grandchildren get accepted into Catholic schools. All did, despite a variety of obstacles. John, a B-29 gunner during World War II, prayed the rosary on every one of his thirty-nine dangerous missions over Japan and returned home safely.

Still others have prayed the rosary as a sheer act of love. According to those close to him, Padre Pio, an Italian Capuchin monk who died in 1968, was said to have prayed the rosary constantly, up to thirty-five times a day. Padre Pio prayed for the conversion of sinners and for all those who requested his prayers. He often said, "Love the Madonna and pray the rosary, for her rosary is the weapon against the evils of the world today." Many healings have been attributed to his intercessory prayer.

For countless people, the rosary has become a central element in their prayer life, serving many purposes—personal spiritual growth, intercessory prayer, healing, and contemplative prayer among them. These people are saints, laypersons, religious, parents, singles, children, and even non-Catholics.

Still, there are cultural and historical reasons for resistance to rosary meditation. American culture tends to place extreme trust in the power of the intellect. The rosary sounds a wrong note; it seems anti-intellectual. This was a particular problem for me when I began to think about saying the rosary as an adult. But I found that my intellectual preoccupations were contributing to the problem, not helping to relieve it. I believed that I would be saved if I just *knew* enough, just filled my brain with enough knowledge. Such a distorted outlook kept my brain frenzied and my spirit in turmoil.

Now I say the rosary because it helps me to enter into deeper stillness where my intellect alone cannot take me. As with most prayer, it works simply because it does, not because I *understand* how it works. In his book *A Western Way of Meditation: The Rosary Revisited,* David Burton Byran draws an analogy between the mysteries of prayer and the mysteries of science.

> The greatest discoveries of physics (relativity and quantum mechanics, for example) are but imperfectly understood, even by great physicists. But however imperfectly understood, these discoveries are effectively used in the uncovering of further truths and in the design of new techniques and inventions. Using these discoveries helps to appreciate them. It would be sophomoric to deny the new discoveries simply because their deepest meaning continually eludes us.

Clearly, we were not meant to live on intellect alone. War, disease, and other social, economic, and environmental problems have all flourished in this enlightened, technologically advanced age. We can e-mail over oceans in seconds and use satellites to track weather in distant lands we will never visit— yet we've never struggled more with isolation and loneliness. Rosary meditation is an opportunity to shed intellectual, emotional, and physical restrictions and to tap into a spiritual relationship that has no limits—the kind of connection that tells us who we are and sustains lasting peace, the kind of connection intrinsic to our nature as human beings with eternal souls.

The rosary reflects the divine order of things, a hierarchy within which science, natural law, mathematics, and the arts all find their proper places. A person who prays the rosary becomes aware of the order of things: problems don't seem so big, and God doesn't seem so distant or indifferent. Any meditation is really a call-and-response, an action and reaction, an attempt to connect two divided parties—the meditator and God—all within God's divine order and purpose. When we make that connection, transformation can begin to take place, change can be effected, and peace of mind has a place to grow.

Why the rosary? It's tempting to say, "Why not?" and leave it at that. Instead, I suggest that you may find your answer in the experiences of others who have asked the same question and, like children, helpless to their need for connection, have proceeded forward without understanding entirely why.

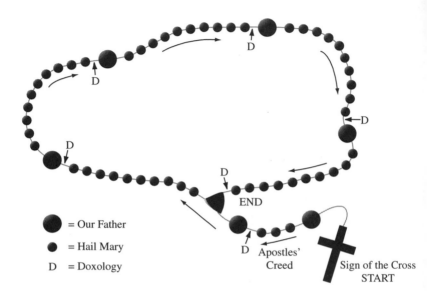

Begin the rosary with the sign of the cross, followed by the recitation of the Apostles' Creed. Then follow the beads down the pendent. On the first bead, announce the mystery and say an Our Father; on each of the next three beads say a Hail Mary. In the space that follows, recite the doxology. The next bead begins the body of the rosary pattern: an Our Father on the first large bead followed by ten Hail Marys on the next ten beads and the doxology in the following space. Repeat that pattern throughout the rest of the rosary. At the beginning of each decade, announce a mystery. You may pause for a moment and think about the meaning of that mystery and then continue on with the rest of the decade.

What Is the Rosary?

The rosary, like anything that has spanned centuries, has had a richly complex evolution. It has borrowed from many traditions and has been influenced by many people. It has been prayed in a variety of ways and continues to spawn variations and inspire supplements. But the traditional rosary is a simple thing, a devotional tool that teaches through prayerful meditation the life, death, and resurrection of Christ. The *Catechism* calls the rosary the "epitome of the whole Gospel." It is a scriptural meditation; eighteen of the twenty mysteries, or meditations, are drawn directly from the New Testament. The person praying the rosary repeats several common Catholic prayers and uses the beads to help him or her keep track of both the meditation and the prayer. The rosary works on multiple levels: it is a physical object; it involves the intellect and the imagination in meditation; and its purpose is developing spiritual insight and, ultimately, connection with God.

The mysteries of the contemporary rosary focus on Christ's early life, public life, passion, death, and resurrection. However, because most of the rosary prayers are Hail Marys and because two of the mysteries are dedicated to Marian events, the rosary sometimes appears to be focused on Mary rather than on Christ. Thus people sometimes ask if Catholics are worshiping Mary and want to know what it means to pray to Mary. *Why would people ask Mary to pray for them?* they wonder. This question will be addressed in detail in chapter 3. For now, I would just like to point out that the focus of the rosary is on Christ. This will become clearer as we take a more concentrated look at the evolution of the rosary as a devotional tool.

We must keep in mind three major histories when considering the development of the rosary: the prayers themselves and their origins; the actual physical rosary (beads, chain, and crucifix); and the addition of the mysteries. All three elements developed in combination with each other to finally make up the rosary we know today.

> "The rosary provides me with so many opportunities to connect with God. There's the physical part, moving the beads through the fingers; the vocal prayer; and then the mental, meditative reflecting on the scene. The rosary fulfills St. Paul's command that we 'pray without ceasing.'"
>
> Carl, systems analyst

The Prayers of the Rosary

The prayers of the rosary are the Apostles' Creed, the Our Father, the Hail Mary, and the doxology. They make up a conversation with God that essentially follows the pattern of how we greet and respond and communicate with one another.

Imagine being approached by someone who has been standing off in the distance, someone you have been hoping and waiting for. You first note whether the person is male or female; as he or she draws closer you begin to identify other characteristics—eyes, hair, the way the person walks or dresses. Perhaps you recognize the hair, the eyes, and the smile of your mother. As she approaches and greets you, you recognize her voice and observe her gait, which has slowed as she's gotten older. When the two of you embrace, an even more complete experience of her—brown eyes, white hair, gentle, affectionate embrace—fills your senses: "This is my mother who loves me, and I'm happy we are together." You then have a conversation with her about those things that you have in common. You direct your speech and comportment in a way that is appropriate for your mother, for your relationship with her and the history you share together.

This is the experience of the rosary. Prayer is coming to know someone. It creates a common language for communication.

Apostles' Creed

The rosary begins with the recitation of the Apostles' Creed on the crucifix.

I believe in God, the Father almighty, creator of heaven and earth. I believe in Jesus Christ, his only Son, our Lord. He was conceived by the power of the Holy Spirit and born of the Virgin Mary. He suffered under Pontius Pilate, was crucified, died, and was buried. He descended to the dead. On the third day he rose again. He ascended into heaven, and is seated at the right hand of the Father. He will come again to judge the living and the dead. I believe in the Holy Spirit, the holy catholic Church, the communion of saints, the forgiveness of sins, the resurrection of the body, and the life everlasting. Amen.

Derived from the Nicene Creed, the Apostles' Creed is a declaration of the basic tenets of the faith. It reflects and prepares us for the coming meditations. It serves a communal purpose by establishing a common language of faith for all those who may be praying the rosary. It also serves a personal faith-fortifying purpose by allowing us to declare our faith vocally and by reminding us of the signal characteristics of our triune God.

Our Father

The Our Father, or the Lord's Prayer, follows the creed. It is recited on the first bead and introduces each decade, or group of ten Hail Marys.

Our Father, who art in heaven, hallowed be thy name; thy kingdom come; thy will be done on earth as it is in heaven. Give us this day our daily bread; and forgive us our trespasses as we forgive those who trespass against us; and lead us not into temptation, but deliver us from evil. Amen.

Given to us from the lips of Christ himself, the Our Father is the most important prayer in the entire devotion. Because it is taken directly from Scripture, the Our Father has a simple history, but its meaning is certainly rich. Space does not allow for a lengthy study of the prayer, but a brief overview will help place it in the proper context. You may find it helpful to consult some of the many commentaries and devotional books that discuss the Lord's Prayer.

Our Father, who art in heaven, hallowed be thy name: We begin by identifying the one being addressed: our Father. We recognize other characteristics of his nature: he is of a divine, or heavenly, nature. Thus he is worthy of praise—his name is holy, honored, and uniquely his. With these basic characteristics in mind, we have become aware of the one to whom we are speaking, and we will conduct ourselves accordingly.

The Our Father remains significant for many reasons. Christ taught us to address God in the most personal way imaginable, as *Abba*—a word close to "Papa" or "Dad." This emphasizes the intimacy of Christ's relationship to God, and by teaching his disciples to pray in this manner, Christ was inviting us to enjoy the same intimacy. The Our Father, then, is a constant reminder of our childlike dependence on God and of the profound level of intimacy into which he invites us. But addressing God as Father was also problematic and would continue to be throughout early church history. For example, during the rule of the Romans, the Our Father was considered subversive because it addressed God as Father rather than as emperor.

Thy kingdom come; thy will be done on earth as it is in heaven: The next phrase of the Our Father continues the process of recognition and begins the transition into petition. We recognize that, because God is our Father, his kingdom will be established and his will will be enacted in our earthly lives, just as his will is the central cause and meaning of heaven. This part of the prayer also expresses our desire that the order of heaven come and visit the earth. We make a conscious choice to bend our will to God's and to join our plans with his, rather than the other way around.

Give us this day our daily bread: Because God is our Father, we come with confidence to ask him to provide for all our needs—physical, mental, emotional, and spiritual. The emphasis here on "this day" should not be overlooked; we ask for God's provision for this day and this day only. By doing so, we choose to leave our future needs completely in God's hands, trusting that his word is true and that we need not worry about tomorrow, for "tomorrow will bring worries of its own. Today's trouble is enough for today" (Matthew 6:34). In other words, Christ is reminding us that we do not need to borrow trouble we don't have.

Furthermore, there is an obvious link between "daily bread" and the Last Supper. The daily bread we now celebrate is the Eucharist at Mass.

And forgive us our trespasses as we forgive those who trespass against us: We've already asked for God's provision; now we request his forgiveness. To trespass essentially means to sin against or violate someone else. We have injured and been injured by others, but we ardently seek to forgive as we have been forgiven. A contrite heart is essential to communion with God. Forgiving and forgiveness go hand in hand. As it is repeated throughout the rosary, the Our Father offers us multiple opportunities to reconcile ourselves to God, ourselves, and others.

And lead us not into temptation, but deliver us from evil. Amen: Finally, we ask that God make one last provision: to protect us against temptation and evil in whatever form it may take in our lives. Saying "Amen" is simply another way of saying "I believe" or "So be it."

The Our Father is a beautiful, complete prayer, but it can be difficult to say. To ask for God's will and not your own; to concern yourself with this day only and not worry about what the future may hold; to be forgiving, even of those who persecute you and cause you pain—all this takes effort that goes against our human grain. We continually struggle to recognize God as our Father, as the source of our life and the one completely dedicated to our well-being.

Doxology

Glory to the Father, and to the Son, and to the Holy Spirit: as it was in the beginning, is now, and will be forever. Amen.

The doxology, a simple prayer of praise, follows each decade of Hail Mary prayers and is the continuation of the Our Father.

Glory to the Father, and to the Son, and to the Holy Spirit: Because we recognize God and the ways in which he has created us, provided for us, and saved us, we praise him in his triune nature as Father, Son, and Holy Spirit.

As it was in the beginning, is now, and will be forever. Amen: This phrase captures another characteristic of God and his kingdom: they are eternal, never changing. He is above and beyond time in ways we cannot comprehend. But we can rest assured that because of his eternal, never-changing nature, he *is* and is available to us for eternity.

Hail Mary

Hail Mary, full of grace, the Lord is with you. Blessed are you among women, and blessed is the fruit of your womb, Jesus. Holy Mary, Mother of God, pray for us sinners, now and at the hour of our death. Amen.

The Hail Mary is recited on each of the ten beads between the Our Father and the doxology. Rosary meditation, like all Marian devotion, hinges on the angelic salutation "Greetings, favored one! The Lord is with you" (Luke 1:28). God enters human history in a unique way through the Incarnation at this specific point, with this specific address to this specific girl. The angel's words introduce Mary into the Gospels and begin the Hail Mary, but the Hail Mary is not the first prayer addressed to Mary, historically speaking.

The earliest Marian prayer we know about was written in Egypt in the third century. It is called Sub Tuum Praesidium: "Under your mercy we take refuge, O Mother of God. Do not reject our supplications in necessity, but deliver us from danger, [O you] alone pure and alone blessed." Clearly, this early prayer had already delineated a number of important characteristics of Mary's role in the church and in prayer.

Under your mercy we take refuge, O Mother of God: This address asserts that Christ is indeed divine; it is not an attempt to assign to Mary the divinity that is reserved solely for God. But because she is the mother of the wholly human, wholly divine Jesus, Mary's relationship with Christ is especially intimate and blessed. It places her particularly close to him, like any mother to her child.

Do not reject our supplications in necessity, but deliver us from danger: This portion of the earliest Marian prayer is obviously modeled after the Our Father. The intention is not so much to glorify Mary as to point out her special role as intercessor. As the last portion of the prayer points out—"[O you] alone pure and alone blessed"—no one else was chosen to carry Christ. No one else had been prepared with enough purity to bear the Incarnation.

This early Marian prayer contains the general sentiment of the present-day Hail Mary:

Hail Mary, full of grace, the Lord is with you: The angelic salutation is taken directly from the New Testament, Luke 1:28. It is spoken in a moment of recognition. The angel calls Mary "full of grace" because he recognizes her as the one God has chosen, the one he has been developing—not only since her own earthly conception but since the beginning of time—as the vessel for the Messiah.

Blessed are you among women, and blessed is the fruit of your womb, Jesus: This portion of the prayer is also taken from Scripture, Luke 1:42, during Mary's visit to Elizabeth. Elizabeth greets Mary with these words, calling her blessed because the fruit of her womb is Jesus, the Messiah. Mary is blessed not through any merit of her own, but because she has been chosen by God. Jesus' name was added during the development of this prayer, probably during the thirteenth century. Not only is the word *Jesus* physically central to the prayer, it is also spiritually central to it, as it is in all Marian devotion.

Holy Mary, Mother of God: "Holy Mary" is self-explanatory. The Messiah entered human history in a vessel prepared for him by God, a vessel that is therefore holy. The title "Mother of God" is a commentary on the role of Christ among us. Mary was declared *Theotokos,* or "Mother of God," at the Council of Ephesus in AD 431. This went against the Nestorian heresy, which suggested that Christ was not one divine person but a human person joined to the divine person of God's Son. The title "Mother of God" tells us unequivocally that Christ is at the same time fully divine and fully human—"true God and true Man" "born according to the flesh," according to the *Catechism*. There is evidence that "Mother of God" was added to the prayer around the fourteenth century.

Pray for us sinners, now and at the hour of our death. Amen: We ask Mary to intercede for us, to pray for us, because she is the honored mother of God and her prayers are invaluable. Furthermore, we ask that in the same way that she endured and suffered with her Son while he was dying on the cross, a witness and a source of comfort until his final breath, she be with us when we die—leading us, as the *Catechism* says, "to her Son, Jesus, in paradise."

The Hail Mary prayer has been in development since the earliest days of the church. The prayer's present form was not established until 1568, when it, along with the Our Father, was added to the published Roman Breviary. At the time of its inclusion in the Breviary, it was not necessarily intended for use in rosary meditation. The popularity of the Hail Mary and the rosary in general soared thanks to the efforts of men like St. Dominic, a missionary who lived in southern France during the thirteenth century, and others who had a deep personal devotion to Mary.

Pier's Secret Life

Blessed Pier Giorgio Frassati (1901–1925) was young, handsome, popular, well educated, and wealthy. He was also remarkably devoted to the rosary.

Beloved especially among young people and among university students in particular, Blessed Pier Giorgio was an extraordinary young person who had the fervent prayer life of a mystic. As the son of a socially prominent Italian businessman and politician, Pier Giorgio was a member of the Turinese elite. He was as rigorous and ardent about his athletic life as he was about his prayer life; hiking, horseback riding, mountain climbing, skiing, and bicycling were some of his favorite activities. He often attended the theater and was fond of art, literature, and music. Behind the scenes, however, lived a different Pier Giorgio.

His secret life as an extraordinarily generous and humble servant to the poor began to be revealed after his death from polio at age twenty-four. Pier Giorgio most likely contracted the disease when he was visiting the sick. When his funeral was held, the streets of Turin were filled with mourners, many of them the poor, sick, lonely, and aged that Pier Giorgio had helped throughout his short life. He sacrificed much to help Turin's downtrodden, such as when he took all the money his father had given him at his graduation and gave it to the poor. Even on his deathbed, he offered instructions to his friends and family about how to care for the poor who had come to depend upon him. Much to the surprise of even his own family, Pier Giorgio had impacted the lives of thousands of the faceless poor of Turin.

Pier Giorgio's inner life was rich as well. He often spent the night in the tabernacle, kneeling before the Eucharist in profound prayer. He belonged to a nocturnal eucharistic adoration group and was one of the most devoted members. One of his favorite prayers was the rosary. He even cultivated plants whose seeds he would use to make rosaries for his friends. His rosary was always with him, either encircling his hand as he walked to and from church or hiked up mountains, or in his pocket, to be retrieved at any moment. In the final years of his life, Pier Giorgio prayed the full fifteen mysteries daily and was a steadfast promoter of the rosary, something that did not always draw favorable attention. While he was entirely silent about his help to the poor, he was sometimes criticized for being an exhibitionist with regard to his rosary devotion. But those who criticized him were often won over in time.

Pier Giorgio was beatified by Pope John Paul II in 1990. During the process, numerous testimonies were gathered from those who knew him. These testimonies have been collected by his niece, Wanda Gawronska, of the Associazione Pier Giorgio Frassati. In these testimonies, many remarked on the attentiveness with which Pier Giorgio recited the prayers of the rosary, a devotion that inspired all who were aware of it. Anne Deppe Rahner, sister of eminent theologian Karl Rahner, S.J., said that on the first night she and her family met Pier Giorgio, he prayed the rosary in his bedroom. The family was deeply touched. Fr. Rahner later remarked that "I was amazed when he recited the rosary aloud in his room. I could not understand it at the time. A youngster from our time had to have a beautiful piety first in order to then love the rosary as much as he did."

Pier Giorgio's love for the rosary and the Eucharist was accompanied by a great simplicity of faith in action. He would offer the coat off his back to someone without one; he fed the hungry and housed the homeless. He led a positive, simple, faithful life, and this was the measure of his sanctity. Recently exhumed as part of the canonization process, Blessed Pier Giorgio's body was found incorrupt, a sign of his great purity, piety, and faith.

The Physical Rosary

Beads, knotted cords, ropes, chains, and other tallying devices have been used in prayer for centuries, not only by Christians, but by religious believers of all kinds—such as Buddhists, Hindus, and Muslims. In the Middle Ages, Christians began to say 150 Our Fathers as a substitute for the 150 psalms that priests said in the Divine Office, using beads as a way to keep track of the prayers. Sometimes they gathered 150 stones and cast one away with each prayer. In the late Middle Ages, the Hail Mary replaced the Our Father in the daily recitation of 150 prayers—a devotion called the Marian Psalter. When the traditional rosary came into use, the Our Father was once again included in the meditation, claiming an appropriate place at the beginning of each decade.

At different points in its development, the rosary was a simple long cord that had 150 knots, and at other times it had only 50. The tallying devices of early rosaries were made from whatever material was on hand, including apricot or olive pits, bone, wood, stones, or pebbles. As the rosary developed in the fifteenth and sixteenth centuries, metalsmiths began mass-producing rosaries using glass, pewter, lead, and iron. Beginning in the eighteenth century, women would sometimes adorn their rosary chains or cords with figurines, dried flowers, gems, even dried fruit. Eventually, the crucifix was added to the rosary and reserved for the recitation of the Apostles' Creed. The crucifix and the first five beads make up the pendent. The first three Hail Marys were added as a petition for faith, hope, and charity. In calling upon these virtues at the beginning of each rosary, we are calling upon the same Holy Spirit that over-shadowed Mary, the same Holy Spirit we call upon at every Mass and in all the sacraments.

"God is the best psychologist. He gave us the rosary because we're body and soul and we need something to grab onto physically. You need something to help keep you focused."

Fr. Anthony Anderson, pastor

The Mysteries of the Rosary

In the Middle Ages, a meditation on some event in the life of Jesus or Mary was paired with each of the 150 prayers in the Psalter that eventually became the rosary. These events were drawn from Scripture, but they were not necessarily direct quotes. They helped the praying person focus on a particular virtue. They were also a means of teaching the gospel to a culture that had few books. Even today, some people pray a Scripture verse for each bead of the rosary. The rosary of St. Dominic was probably most like the scriptural rosary. During the Renaissance, picture rosaries became very popular. These rosaries were accompanied by small paintings on wood of the various mysteries. To make the pictures more manageable, the 150 meditations were reduced to the fifteen mysteries we have today. In 1569, Pope Pius V officially recognized fifteen mysteries, separated into three groups:

- *The joyful mysteries.* The Annunciation, the Visitation, the birth of Jesus, the presentation of Jesus, and the finding of Jesus in the temple

- *The sorrowful mysteries.* The agony in the garden, the scourging at the pillar, the crowning with thorns, the carrying of the cross, and the crucifixion and death of Jesus

- *The glorious mysteries.* The Resurrection, the Ascension, the descent of the Holy Spirit, the assumption of Mary, and the coronation of Mary

As further evidence that the rosary is an evolving meditation, in 2002, Pope John Paul II declared the year of 2003 the Year of the Rosary. In celebration of this pronouncement, he recognized the luminous mysteries, five events from the public life of Jesus' ministry.

- *The luminous mysteries.* The baptism of Jesus in the Jordan, the first miracle at the wedding feast of Cana, the proclamation of the kingdom, the Transfiguration, and the institution of the Eucharist in the last supper.

It is likely that these mysteries were selected not just for their spiritual merit but also because they could be easily visualized. This made them effective tools for teaching the life of Christ and Mary to people who could not read. Their pictorial quality also makes them suitable for prayerful meditation. At present, a rosary devotee can choose to meditate on any one of many beautiful mysteries.

For instance, one may chose to meditate on the mysteries of the Beatitudes. In this version, the traditional mysteries are replaced with the Beatitudes from Christ's Sermon on the Mount (Matthew 5:1–12). The meditator recalls one beatitude for each decade: "Blessed are the poor in spirit, for theirs is the kingdom of heaven"; "Blessed are those who mourn, for they will be comforted"; "Blessed are the meek, for they will inherit the earth"; and so on. Other variations on the rosary concentrate on such topics as the Eucharist, the work of the Holy Spirit, the sacraments, motherhood, fatherhood, and healing.

"The words are a kind of melody which soothes the ear and isolates us from the noise of the world around us, the fingers being occupied meanwhile in allowing one bead after another to slip through. Thus the imagination is kept tranquil and the mind and will are set free to be united to God."

Reginald Garrigou-Lagrange, theologian

The Rosary and the Church

Rosary devotion is entirely optional for Catholics, yet it continues to be very popular. The rosary is a flexible instrument for meditation. Its prayers and mysteries are quite fluid, and many different forms of the rosary exist to help foster the devotee's spiritual life. Devotions in general are a potent means to developing one's faith, but a person doesn't have to practice rosary devotion in order to be a practicing, faithful Catholic.

Nevertheless, Catholic saints and pastors have frequently urged people to pray the rosary. One of the first of these was St. Dominic, who believed that praying the rosary was a way to reach hardened souls who'd gone astray from the teaching of the church. He believed that by praying the rosary they could be won over to God.

Rosary devotion has been an enormous part of the devotional life of many of the clergy and has garnered much attention from many popes, especially Pope John Paul II. Numerous encyclicals have been written about the rosary. Pope Leo XIII alone wrote thirteen, and the rosary is mentioned in many others, offering substantial support for rosary devotion as a means to bringing the church together and individuals closer to God.

In recent years, people have been encouraged to personalize their private rosary meditation so that it becomes most efficacious for them. Outside of the Mass, it's one of the best communal prayers for families. It is simple to learn, and many excellent materials on rosary devotion are now available for children.

The rosary is a history lesson, a study in theology, and a simple meditative prayer all in one. When you pick up rosary beads, it's like you're picking up the gospel. When you pray the rosary, it's like you're taking the hand of Christ and walking through his life with him and his mother, Mary. And she, so close to him, had quite a spectacular view.

The Rosary Then and Now

My wounds will repair yours.
—Blessed Sr. Mary Martha Chambon

I came to this task of writing about the rosary with some degree of trepidation. I'm hardly an example of prayerful piety—the course of my rosary devotion has been about as focused as the travels of a housefly: fit to short bursts of buzzing here and there and everywhere, at no one place for too long. On the other hand, my experience is hardly unique. And I can testify that rosary meditation is a powerful spiritual tool—even for someone with a scattered and inconsistent devotional past.

In my family, rosary devotion was practiced primarily by my mother, whose name, appropriately enough, is Mary. On Christmas Eve, she would gather us all together in front of the enormous Nativity scene my father had built out of scraps of barn wood. Before we opened our presents (which were abundant with nine people in our family) my father would lead us all in the rosary. This moment, one of the most peaceful in our house all year long, is a fond memory for me. The whole family was together, preparing for this great celebration by recalling the joyful mysteries and remembering first and foremost the reason for Christmas. I must admit, however, that while I was praying, my thoughts would wander toward the presents waiting under the tree. Although I was fond of the rosary, I wasn't exactly a skilled meditator at the time.

Growing up Catholic, I never thought it odd that we asked Mary to pray for us. I always imagined her in heaven, somewhere in the vicinity of her Son. Jesus, of course, would be obligated to follow the commandments and honor his own earthly mother, even in heaven. So it was never a big stretch for me to imagine her hearing my prayers, then leaning across heaven's great feasting table and saying, just as she did at the wedding feast of Cana, "Oh, Son, there's something I'd like to call to your attention." Nor was it a stretch to think of Christ as an essential part of the devotion. Most of the rosary is spent meditating on the events of his life, so it never seemed to me that the focus of the rosary was anywhere but on the mystery of the Son of man. And as far as I knew, Jesus was absolutely my friend, every bit as accessible as anyone else in heaven.

As a young child, I would take long walks along a path behind our house where violets and Dutchman's-breeches grew in abundance. I would pick flowers and talk to Jesus, Mary, and Joseph. I was deeply enamored with the holy family and thought of them as I thought of my own family. I always felt in some way that I had been chosen by Mary, that I had been assigned, as she had been, some special task to accomplish for the Father.

This sense of designation got a big boost in first grade when I was selected to carry the crown for the May crowning, a tradition that celebrates Mary's being crowned Queen of Heaven and Earth. The girls in the ceremony wore handmade dresses that resembled the bride and bridesmaids' dresses in a wedding. The blue bride's dress was reserved for the girl selected to carry Mary's crown on a little silk pillow in the procession. That year, I was the privileged "bride." The other girls seemed to think that the only reason I was selected for this honored position was that the dress happened to fit me. I believed (and still do!) that Mary had chosen me. She was already speaking to me about the work that she had for me to do on the planet.

As I walked down the aisle in my little blue dress, a wreath of flowers on my head, I thought about Mary, about how much I loved her and how the thought of her simply made me smile. To be honest, I loved being the center of attention. It was a rare spot indeed for a girl who was one of the youngest in a family of seven children, and I was thoroughly enjoying my brief reign. When I reached the front of the church, I turned at the aisle to approach the "crowner," a sixth-grader who was the tallest in her class and therefore selected for the task. But as I turned, the little crown of flowers slid off the slippery silk pillow and landed gently on the floor.

Others in the ceremony were obviously annoyed by the slip, but I sensed nothing irreverent or errant about it. I simply bent down, picked up the crown, placed it back on the pillow, and held it out to the sixth-grader, who was by then sneering at me in my imperfection. But it was as if Mary was saying to me even in that moment, "It's all right, my child. These things happen. Just pick it up and move right on."

Over the years, this has been a part of the continual conversation between Mary and me. "It's all right," she says. "Just pick up and move on."

My rosary devotion came and went through the years as I dipped into other religions, agnosticism, and radical feminism and experienced a variety of dark nights of the soul. I left my rosary devotion behind in my first year of college, when I lived next door to two southern "Bible-Belters" who convinced me with their dazzling recall of Scripture that I was surely no Christian because I was Catholic. They would look at the crucifix around my neck and say, "Haven't you heard? He rose from the dead—he's not on the cross anymore." Slowly but surely, out of my own ignorance and deficient religious training, I began to drop my devotion to all things Catholic.

For several years I faithfully attended Protestant churches and Bible studies, where I learned to pray the Scriptures. I knew the rosary to be a Scripture-based meditation, but I did not pray it during this period. The problem was that all of my prayers seemed fruitless. I couldn't quiet myself enough to pray. I lacked and longed for clarity of thought. I couldn't seem to penetrate my emotional-intellectual-spiritual fog long enough to reach those quiet, contemplative places where God had really spoken to me in the past. I ached in my heart for the simplicity of the times when I walked with and talked to the holy family while picking flowers behind my house.

I briefly picked up the rosary again following a pilgrimage I made during my first year of graduate school. But for the most part I only had fond, ever-dimming memories of saying the rosary with my family as a child. I had no real understanding of what the rosary was or what it could do for me.

Meanwhile, I spiraled downward emotionally. I was ignoring much pain—pain from past abuses and past relationships, pain from my frustrations and anxieties in the present—and trying to forget. Most significant, I wanted to forget that I had been raped a number of years earlier and had never told anyone. It was as though my mind had flipped on a switch to a neon light that kept flashing through my brain, "That didn't happen." But what my mind tried desperately to forget, my body and spirit could not. I felt crushed, confused, soulless.

I medicated that pain as best I could. I ate too much or not at all. I ran compulsively until I ruined my knees. Then I started gluing myself to the television for hours each night. I gradually rendered myself completely debilitated by what could only be described as addiction. Nothing kept at bay the still darker demons waiting for me: raging loneliness, self-pity, resentment. To say that my life was not working would be a gross understatement. I was depressed, barely able to function in the professional world, and growing further and further isolated. So much repressed anguish was now gushing forth in one long, drawn-out, murky cry that I didn't know what to do. I thought I might be losing my mind. Maybe I was not far from it.

That's where rosary meditation finally found me—sinking under the oppressive weight of unaddressed personal wounds that I carried in silence and secrecy. I wanted peace, but I knew I couldn't reach silence, much less contemplation, until I'd addressed my past with God, with others, and with myself. But God felt unfathomably far away, well out of earshot of my supplications. In despair, I turned to the rosary. In my emotional and spiritual turmoil, I could pray no other way.

I started going to daily Mass. At church I met someone who told me about a little chapel that could be used twenty-four hours a day if you knew the code to the door. She gave me the code, and I started going there, sometimes for up to four hours a visit, late at night while few other people were there. I didn't know what to make of it all, but I also sensed that I needed to be in that chapel for as many hours out of the day as possible. Something was there for me, hidden in that silent, holy place. I could not have expressed it at the time, but it was peace. And the rosary, as it turns out, was the catalyst to my arriving in those silent places where God could begin to do his healing work in me.

I couldn't pray in familiar ways. I couldn't write, which had always been my first form of prayer. So at first I just came to the chapel and sat and looked around. At the back of the sanctuary was a statue of Mary with candles at her feet to be lit as reminders of special intentions. Something about that little nook struck me, drew me in. I was comfortable there, in the warmth of those candles, in the gentle invitation of Mary's outstretched arms. Mary didn't seem to mind my little slipup with her crown when I was a child, and she didn't seem to mind the more serious slipups I'd been making since then. It was as if she was consoling me once again: "It's all right, child. Things happen. Just pick up where you left off."

Then I started to pray the rosary—it was the only prayer associated with Mary that I remembered. It was easy and restful because I'd memorized the prayers, and that meant that I didn't have to think too much. In the beginning, I didn't concern myself too deeply with the meditations on the mysteries. Instead, I simply announced them and moved into the prayers of the decade. I was relieved by the rosary's simplicity and uniformity. As a former runner, I found the repetition of the prayers comforting. Something in that simple repetition lent itself to transcendence. It was like the runner's high I'd felt during long, hard workouts, when my brain could rest and my body could absorb itself in its strenuous task. The rosary silenced the craziness in my head and heart. I began to cling to it as a drowning person clutches a life preserver without a lot of conscious thought. I even wore a rosary around my neck in an almost literal hope that it would keep me from sinking.

Little did I know that those beads held a transforming power. Little did I know that I was reaching out for the ultimate human intercessor. Mary, like any devoted prayer partner, would stand in the gap that loomed between God and me. And because "the prayer of the righteous is powerful and effective" (James 5:16), Mary, so devoted and so close to her Son, must surely have his ear.

In part, I ran to Mary because she is female, a human being who in some manner would better understand the kind of violation I had suffered. But this was only part of why I ran to her. I was also drawn to the rosary because one full third of it focused on the sorrowful mysteries—the agony in the garden, the scourging at the pillar, the crowning with thorns, the carrying of the cross, and the crucifixion and death of Jesus. (The luminous mysteries had not yet been officially recognized as a part of the meditation.) Although the sorrowful mysteries were never my favorite mysteries as a child, now I had a new understanding of just how brutal and visceral these wounds were. And I ran to the rosary because the glorious mysteries followed the sorrowful. That perfect balance of joy, sorrow, and glory— their order, constancy, and vivid simplicity—brought me a promise of peace.

Of course, most of this was hardly a conscious thought in my brain at the time. Only years later, after much intervention, countless hours of prayer and support, and change brought about through intercessory prayer, can I look back on that time and say, "No wonder." In that gentle, repetitious cry—"pray for us"—my heart and mind, once frenzied by emotion, began to grow very still, still enough to speak to God with honesty, still enough to listen.

The rosary and a variation called the Rosary to the Holy Wounds have given me some of the most powerful—and sometimes painful—experiences of prayer as well as some of the most intimate, real experiences of God I've ever had. They have taught me that it's never too late to just "pick up where you left off and keep moving." They have taught me the rewards of a daily spiritual life, of daily seeking the spiritual disciplines. I have learned that real change comes about through the grace of God and because God chooses me, not because I somehow become perfect. I have learned that even when the best of my efforts look like that buzzing housefly—scattered, short-lived, and frenzied—God is willing to meet me right where I am and do for me what I cannot do for myself.

Like so many who pray the rosary, I will never be able to explain it fully. I only know my own experience and the experiences of others I have learned about along the way, and I am honored to share them with you.

God's nature is mysterious—not mysterious as in a puzzle to be solved, but in how he embraces us in our uniqueness. His mystery allows us to be still and rest assured that while we do not have all the answers, there is one who is greater than we are who does. In this way, the mysteries of the rosary have not been a source of befuddlement or estrangement or shame over my own inadequacy as much as a source of comfort, a place whereby I can measure my rightful place in the universe. That too is a mystery. Scripture tells me that I am simultaneously dust (Genesis 3:19) and the apple of my Father's eye (Deuteronomy 32:10). In that knowledge I can rest in peaceful awe and clarity, the goal of any meditation.

The Art of Devotion

Not everyone who develops a taste for rosary devotion was raised on it. In fact, many who come to rosary meditation have taken a far more unlikely route.

Singer-songwriter Kate Campbell, a practicing Southern Baptist, is one such example. She is the daughter of a Southern Baptist preacher, was born and raised in the South, and is married to a Baptist chaplain. Just shy of a doctorate in southern history, she says that it is through the study of southern history that she has been able to come to grips with southern culture in all of its beauty, gentility, faith, violence, and conflict. She also says that it was through her practice of rosary meditation that she began to understand the meaning of devotion.

Inspired by her own rosary devotion, Campbell assembled a collection of southern tales about the lost art of devotion set to Americana-style music in *Rosaryville,* her fourth album. The centerpiece of the album, "Heart of Hearts," is about a man who makes a rosary in his yard with bowling balls.

"Even though I was raised Baptist," says Campbell, "I've always had one really good friend who was Catholic. Once or twice a year I would go to Mass, and my father would allow that. I'm not sure that all Baptist preachers would allow their daughters to attend a Mass. But my father was always very open about that."

She developed a natural curiosity about Catholicism and was particularly drawn to the liturgy and the rosary because she couldn't find anything comparable in her religious tradition.

"I was very drawn to the mysticism and . . . I had always been fascinated with the rosary. I'd always wondered what the purpose of it was, so I read a book called *The History of the Rosary* and got some rosary beads and started saying the rosary."

The rosary began to fill a void that Campbell had felt in her devotional life. She was drawn to it not only for its history and the comfort she received from it but also for the quiet picture of devotion that was beginning to form in her mind. And it challenged her understanding of Mary's role.

"[As a Protestant], basically all you're told all your life about Catholics is that they worship Mary. When I started reading about the rosary, [I realized it] was not about worshipping Mary, but about a way of increasing your own devotional life, and that the rosary really was intended to bring you closer to Christ."

Rosary meditation also resonated for Campbell on a feminine level.

"I think there is something very powerful about the words, 'Hail Mary, full of grace, the Lord is with thee. Blessed art thou among women.' To me, as a woman, this does not take away from the divinity of Christ but continues to remind us that Christ was born of a woman. . . . And maybe it's the feminine side of Christ that we overlook. . . . It's a very strong statement for women."

Rosaryville is a poignant project in other ways as well. That Campbell should capture devotion in such a wide range of expressions seems salient today, when rosary devotion is appealing more and more to a wider audience, regardless of age or religious affiliation. Campbell seems to recognize most clearly that rosary devotion is a wide umbrella under which all may find shelter. Or, as Campbell says, borrowing a sentiment from an old hymn, "There is a wideness in mercy."

Mary in Our Lives

And then that girl the angels came to visit,
she woke also to fruit, frightened by beauty,
given love, shy, in her
so much blossom, the forest
no one had explored, with paths leading everywhere.

They left her alone to walk and to drift
and the spring carried her along.
Her simple and unselfcentered Mary-life
became marvelous and castlelike.
Her life resembled trumpets on the feast days
that reverberated far inside every house;
and she, once so girlish and fragmented,
was so plunged now inside her womb,
and so full inside from that one thing
and so full—enough for a thousand others—
that every creature seemed to throw light on her
and she was like a slope with vines, heavily bearing.
—Rainer Maria Rilke
  From *Selected Poems of Rainer Maria Rilke*

The rosary is the consummate Marian prayer. It brings us to a deeper relationship with the woman who has stirred more hearts and aroused more controversy than any woman in history. Yet the outstanding fact about devotion to Mary is not that it brings us closer to her, but that, because she exists for her Son, it leads us to Christ.

Even so, or perhaps because this is so, Mary is celebrated, even famous. Great artists have painted her image and sculpted her form. Musicians from Bach to the Beatles have made her the subject of anthems and arias. Poets have tried to pen her essence, philosophers and historians her impact. Her role in the Catholic Church and in the shaping of our culture has been studied and debated for centuries. Despite the passage of two thousand years, she continues to influence our world deeply, this simple Jewish girl whom, as Rilke says, "the angels came to visit."

What makes us want to visit her too?

In 1987, Pope John Paul II predicted that we would see a renewed interest in Mary at the turn of the millennium. He wrote that "Mary appeared on the horizon of salvation history before Christ . . . when 'the fullness of time' was definitively drawing near—the saving advent of Emmanuel—she who was from eternity destined to be his Mother already existed on earth." He went on to say that as we close out the second millennium and come into the third, "it becomes fully comprehensible that in this present period we wish to turn in a special way to her, the one who in the 'night' of the Advent expectation began to shine like a true 'Morning Star.'"

The pope's image of Mary as the morning star is striking and suggestive; and probably better appreciated by past generations. Not only dazzled as we are by the vast beauty of the stars, our ancestors also used the stars for navigation. In their divine alignment, the stars help us find our way. Mary, the morning star, also helps us find our way by directing us to her Son, Jesus, who is "the way, the truth, and the life."

That's what Mary's direction did for me. When I returned to rosary devotion as an adult, I was emotionally bereft and needed someone to stand in the gap between God and me. However, my meager Catholic education had not prepared me to truly know Mary. I knew that she was available to pray for me. I knew that Catholics did not worship her, but venerated her. I was wounded when I sat in Protestant churches or elsewhere and heard Mary spoken of in less than complimentary, even demeaning terms. But I wasn't entirely clear on her role and was embarrassed by the fact that so much time spent in parochial education had failed to make it clear.

When I first returned to the rosary and as I continued to study Catholicism, I came to look upon Mary as a prayer partner. To ask her to pray for me was no different than if I had asked my earthly mother to pray for me. Later, Mary became a kind of sponsor, someone I could turn to who would show me the way, an example of pious living who would show me how to live. The way she showed me took me directly to Christ on the cross. She knew the place well; she had been there at his feet while he died. Over time, the titles "Blessed Mother,"

"mother of God," and "Queen" came to fit her as clearly and comfortably as "mother." But I still had much to discover.

> "This honor given to Mary reveals the dignity of all women; a woman is more important in God's saving plan than any angel or other spiritual being."
>
> Alan Schreck, theologian

Mary in Scripture

I first turned to Scripture. The rosary made it easy for me to focus on the portions of Scripture that clearly involved Mary. Several of the rosary's mysteries are taken from the New Testament accounts of her life and the major events in the life of Christ in which she played a role. These are

- *The Annunciation,* whereby Gabriel invited her to bear the Messiah through the power of the Holy Spirit. She accepted the invitation.

- *The Visitation,* Mary's visit to her cousin Elizabeth. Elizabeth had also been visited by divine intervention, and although it was thought that she was barren, she was also to bear a child.

- *The birth of Jesus* in a stable in Nazareth (also called the Nativity).

- *The presentation of Jesus* by his parents, Mary and Joseph, in the temple according to Jewish law.

- And finally, Mary and Joseph *finding the child Jesus* in the temple after he'd been missing for several days.

These five major events make up the joyful mysteries, which are usually prayed on Mondays. In them, Mary appears in a practical way as mother, friend, the first Christian, and wife. Hers is, in the words of John Paul II, "a presence so discreet as to pass almost unnoticed by the eyes of her contemporaries." The Gospels say nothing more about her until Christ begins his adult ministry. We presume that for all the years in between Mary engaged in the same kind of daily life that any mother might: cleaning and cooking and caring for her family while continuing to cultivate her own spiritual life. It's likely that Mary practiced both contemplation and meditation in her prayer life as well; we are told that she took in the events around her in a meditative way, pondering them in her heart (Luke 2:19, 51).

Mary next appears in Scripture during the wedding feast at Cana, the second luminous mystery. Here a significant characteristic of her role is revealed. When the wedding party runs out of wine, Mary goes to her Son and tells him, "They have no wine" (John 2:3). His response, "Woman, what concern is that to you and to me? My hour has not yet come" (John 2:4), may seem unexpected, but her response is equally weighty. She says to the servants at hand, *"Do whatever he tells you"* (John 2:5, italics mine). And throughout history she consistently says the same thing without wavering for a moment. She draws our attention to Jesus through her example, through her intercession, and through her complete cooperation with and particpation in God's plan of salvation. With total faith in her heart and trust in her Lord, she continually beckons us to "do whatever he tells you."

This message continues through her devoted presence at the foot of the cross. We meditate on the crucifixion and death of her Son in the sorrowful mysteries of the rosary, prayed on Tuesdays and Fridays. They are the agony in the garden, the scourging at the pillar, the crowning with thorns, the carrying of the cross, and the crucifixion and death of Jesus.

Jesus appeared to Mary after his resurrection—the first glorious mystery—and she was present during his ascension and the descent of the Holy Spirit—the second and third glorious mysteries. The same Holy Spirit that overshadowed her during the Annunciation visited her during Pentecost, once again asking her to carry Christ into the world. Only this time, she would not do so physically, but evangelically. Christ was born after the Holy Spirit's first visit to Mary. After the second visit, the church was born. Thus Mary is often called the mother of the church.

Early on in my rediscovery of Mary, I was struck by the notion that God chose a woman to play the most vital role in salvation history aside from that of Christ himself. As Alan Schreck writes, "This honor given to Mary reveals the dignity of all women; a woman is more important in God's saving plan than any angel or other spiritual being." The passive and mournful portrayal of the Madonna that I had seen so often took on a more formidable, tenacious quality.

The Things We Cannot Change

Like most alcoholics and other addicts, Russell was reluctant to accept his condition. It seemed illogical and humiliating to think that he could not control something as seemingly trivial as alcohol.

"It took me a long time to accept the fact that I just couldn't drink like normal people," he says. "That was something I just didn't want to hear."

After a number of years of living with a drinking habit that was clearly out of control, he adopted a practice of "controlled drinking." He had no more than two drinks a day, attended Alcoholics Anonymous meetings for "emotional problems," and convinced himself that his problem wasn't all that serious. It was a dangerous illusion that didn't last long. Eventually, the disease caught up with him, and the desire to drink heavily returned with even greater ferocity.

"I thought I was losing my mind," Russell says. "I thought I had to drink to stay sane. You talk about crazy thinking—that if I *didn't* drink, I was going to lose my mind. But that's the way I felt."

At about this time he returned with more fervor to AA. He also returned to the rosary. He had learned to pray it when he was very young but hadn't given it too much attention since then. It turned out to be an excellent supplement to all that AA taught him about the importance of acceptance and of "keeping it simple." He recognized himself in some of the meditations, such as when he prayed the Annunciation and realized once and for all that he was an alcoholic.

"That to me was like an annunciation," he says, "to finally say that I really was an alcoholic and then accept it. But there are daily annunciations, like when things don't go my way. If I've made the effort for things to go my way and they still don't, I have to accept that and imitate the Blessed Mother. She said, 'Let it be done according to your word,' and that was that. I can try to imitate that. It's easy to say, 'God's will be done,' but that's much harder to do."

Russell says that his favorite mysteries are the sorrowful and that he experiences the most peace while praying them. He uses his rosary devotion primarily as a meditation but also as an intercessory tool when praying for his family. Following each decade, he recites the Serenity Prayer (which AA uses): "God, grant me the serenity to accept the things I cannot change, the courage to change the things I can, and the wisdom to know the difference."

"[The rosary] helps me to get through the world," he says. "It helps me to deal with the world on its own terms rather than really changing my perception of the world. My problem is that I want to be God. But there's only one God, and I'm not him. That's the struggle for me every day. Acceptance is the key."

For Russell, the rosary has been both an example of acceptance—in Mary's "yes" and in Christ's embracing of suffering and of the will of the Father in the sorrowful mysteries—and a means by which he might obtain the grace and serenity of acceptance.

Mary's Silence

The church's understanding of Mary's role does not end with the biblical accounts. It has developed over time through the reflection and contemplation of Scripture. The earliest picture of Mary following those in the Bible comes from the Apostolic Fathers—early Greek Christian authors who, it was thought, were personally acquainted with the original apostles and, presumably, with Mary. Still, these early fathers of the church had relatively little to say about Mary's life and role in the formation of the church. I wondered why. Was it because she was a woman?

In part, the answer may be yes, but not because the Apostolic Fathers were prejudiced. Luigi Gambero, in his work *Mary and the Fathers of the Church,* suggests that the early Christians were wary of placing too much emphasis on Mary because the pagan culture of the time was enamored with feminine deities. Gambero writes that "there was risk that placing stress on the figure of Mary might provoke ambiguous or even erroneous interpretations of her person and her role in relation to Christ." Gambero also invokes what might be called the Ignatian principle of silence. St. Ignatius of Antioch, one of the great figures of the early church, taught that those things Christ did in silence were as worthy of the Father as those things he did in public. Gambero writes that the early church may have applied this principle to Mary in order to "emphasize her mysterious maternal presence in the faith and life of the first Christians: a presence rendered even more intense and intriguing by silence."

The mystical nature of silence has been important in many religious orders for centuries. Trappist monk and writer Thomas Merton said that "the ears with which one hears the message of the Gospel are hidden in man's heart, and these ears do not hear anything unless they are favored with a certain interior solitude and silence." Many religious orders, such as the Missionaries of Charity, practice profound silence—of the eyes, ears, mouth, mind, and heart. As Mother Teresa said, "God is the friend of silence. His language is silence. 'Be still and know that I am God.' He requires us to be silent to discover him. In the silence of the heart, he speaks to us."

Mother Teresa was acutely aware of the silence that Christ practiced and still does. Scripture is silent about most of his early life, he spent forty days in the desert alone (we might assume that much of that was in silence), and now he is silent once more through the Eucharist: "He who spoke with authority now spends his earthly life in silence. Let us adore Jesus in the eucharistic silence." Such silence is a precious commodity in the melee of our culture, where we are starving for silence, eucharistic and otherwise. Fostering an attitude of silence is not about keeping secrets or leaving unsaid things that need to be said; it is not a stoic clamping down. Rather, silence can lead to the most fluid, open, and profound kind of *knowing,* an opportunity, as Mary says in her Magnificat, to magnify the Lord (Luke 1:46). Silence is perhaps the truest recognition of God. In the presence of such holiness, silence is the only appropriate response. As the prophet Habakkuk proclaimed, "the LORD is in his holy temple; let all the earth keep silence before him!" (Habakkuk 2:20). Who better would know and foster this silence than the woman whose own body became his holy temple?

The writings of the early church fathers, then, depict Mary in a perfectly appropriate way. She was simple, humble, pious, and often silent, despite her participation in events that would have caused any person to cry out to the world in agony, fear, and pain. Indeed, the only true calling out she does is in the Magnificat, a song of praise to her Savior. The early church's silence about Mary is not neglect of her role and importance; rather, it's an indication of respect. That silence is a sign that we need to ponder her role and try to understand her choices, which, like her cries, were more often of an internal nature, offered to God and God alone. Her silent example speaks to the precious, private sanctity we all may enjoy in our relationship with God. Her silence flows from a profound intimacy with her Son.

The Assumption and Coronation

The final two glorious mysteries of the rosary are not described in Scripture. They are the assumption of Mary, body and soul, into heaven following her death and the coronation, whereby

Mary is crowned Queen of Heaven and Earth. What do these two mysteries mean? Where did they originate?

They are based on a long history of Marian devotion that began in the earliest days of the church. Such tradition does not contradict the holy Scriptures. Rather, it is developed from the biblical and apostolic faith through the inspiration of the Holy Spirit over a long period of time.

The first mention of Mary's assumption comes from the early church fathers. The church teaches that because Mary lived a virtuous life, one in which she participated freely in God's plan of salvation, she was "taken up body and soul into heavenly glory when her earthly life was over, and exalted by the Lord as Queen over all things." She was granted this honor partly because it was thought that the Messiah would have come to earthly life in a pure vessel. She was also honored because her life was a perfect model of piety and faith. St. Francis de Sales put it simply when he wrote, "In short her heart, her soul, her life were in Heaven; how could she remain long on earth?" The quick redemption of her body is a sign of hope for all believers, a model of what we all may anticipate following a life of faith.

Further argument for the Assumption comes from the lack of a tradition of relics from Mary's body. These would have been highly prized. Traditions of relics from the apostles exist, yet there are none for Jesus' mother. Why not? As the Assumption suggests, there was no body from which relics could have been extracted, because she was invited, through the grace of God, to join her Son: "Rise up, O LORD, and go to your resting place, you and the ark of your might" (Psalm 132:8); "Arise, shine; for your light has come, and the glory of the LORD has risen upon you. . . . I will glorify where my feet rest" (Isaiah 60:1, 13).

Marian devotion during the Middle Ages led to a devotion to Mary's crowning as Queen of Heaven. Fr. Thomas Thompson, director of the Marian Library at the University of Dayton, notes that the idea of Mary's queenship began during the 1400s, an era of general sentimentality regarding royalty. Thus, queenship would have been a natural honor to bestow on a beloved figure.

Scriptural support for the devotion to Mary as queen comes from the many prophetic scriptural citations on Mary, especially Revelation 12:1: "A great portent appeared in heaven: a woman clothed with the sun, with the moon under her feet, and on her head a crown of twelve stars." The Psalms, which were such an important part of the Divine Office and the evolving rosary during this period, also played a role in Mary's title. Psalm 45, for example, celebrates a courtly image:

Hear, O daughter, consider and incline your ear; forget your people and your father's house, and the king will desire your beauty. Since he is your lord, bow to him; the people of Tyre will seek your favor with gifts, the richest of the people with all kinds of wealth. The princess is decked in her chamber with gold-woven robes; in many-colored robes she is led to the king;

behind her the virgins, her companions, follow. With joy and gladness they are led along as they enter the palace of the king. (Psalm 45:10–15)

The Poor Shepherdess and the Beautiful Lady

St. Bernadette of Lourdes is probably the most famous shepherdess in history. Born into poverty in 1844, uneducated and frail with asthma, this poor, simple little girl was visited with an apparition so startling that it changed the world.

Bernadette Soubirous was the firstborn child of Francois and Louise Soubirous, who lived in the village of Lourdes in southern France. The Soubirouses, millers by trade, spent most of their lives in abject poverty, so much so that on three occasions Bernadette's parents sent her to live with others in order to ease the financial burden of feeding a large family. She was an agreeable child in every way, simple and holy, obedient and extremely helpful to her parents because she watched over her younger siblings. She suffered from periodic bouts of asthma but never complained, often taking on arduous tasks that might have placed her health in jeopardy.

During one of those periods that Bernadette spent away from her family, she tended sheep, only returning home when it was decided that she should begin learning the catechism so that she could receive her first communion. She was fourteen. Soon after she returned, on February 11, 1858, while walking in the woods with her sister and a friend, Bernadette heard a strange rushing noise, like the wind or a storm. However, no bushes or trees near her were rustling. The noise came again, and this time she turned toward a grotto where one bush was rustling as though it was very windy. At about the same time, out of the grotto came a golden-colored cloud and soon after a very beautiful lady dressed in white. Bernadette was frightened at first, but the lady, who was more beautiful than anything Bernadette had ever seen, seemed to beckon her. Bernadette kneeled and, with little thought as to what she was doing, began praying her rosary, which she kept in her pocket at all times. The lady, who carried a rosary in her hands, moved the beads through her fingers along with Bernadette but did not pray the Our Father or the Hail Mary. When they came to the doxology, the lady bowed her head and joined in the prayer. Once Bernadette had completed the rosary, the lady smiled and disappeared into the grotto.

This was the first of eighteen apparitions of the lady that Bernadette would experience. During each, the young Bernadette fell into ecstasy. Townspeople thought she might be insane. Authorities even threatened to have her committed, but following each vision Bernadette became radiant. The asthma that had curtailed her activities in the past seemed to bother her less. During the ninth apparition, the lady asked Bernadette to dig in the ground and drink from a spring. The spring that issued from the rocks of the grotto proved to have healing powers. More than sixty miraculous cures attributed to the water at Lourdes have been documented and approved by the church. During the sixteenth apparition, the lady finally revealed her name to the child, who had repeatedly asked her to identify herself. The vision said, "I am the Immaculate Conception."

In 1854, four years earlier, Pope Pius IX had proclaimed the dogma behind the immaculate conception: that Mary remained pure, born without the stain of original sin. It was a dogma that had been developed over centuries of sophisticated study and deep contemplation. The poor, uneducated Bernadette had not heard the title *Immaculate Conception* and did not know what it meant. Another feature of the apparition that serves as an argument for its authenticity is the fact that the lady only prayed the Doxology portion of the rosary— something of theological significance. She would certainly have no need to address herself through the Hail Mary, and the Our Father is a prayer for earthly sinners, not saints in heaven. She would only pray the doxology, a prayer of praise to God.

Bernadette later became a Sister of Charity at the convent at Nevers in France. Like Padre Pio, she often prayed a rosary that she kept in her apron pocket, hiding her devotion to a degree because she didn't want people to misunderstand and speak ill of the Virgin Mary. Like so many devotees, she slept with her rosary, wrapping it around her hand before bed at night. She told a friend to "take your beads and go off to sleep while saying them; do the same as little children who fall asleep saying, 'Mamma, Mamma.'" The rosary was a constant comfort to her, especially during her asthma attacks, when she would press her rosary to her aching chest.

St. Bernadette's experience with the rosary teaches us a valuable lesson about simplicity and piety. Like the Blessed

Mother, she was chosen to receive a remarkable and unique grace, even though she was anonymous, poor, uneducated, and frail. After suffering a long and painful final illness, St. Bernadette died at the age of thirty-five, fulfilling the prophecy of Our Lady of Lourdes, who said during one of the apparitions that Bernadette would die young. Like Pier Giorgio, St. Bernadette was also exhumed during the canonization process and found to be incorrupt.

The apparitions transformed Lourdes into a popular pilgrimage spot that today draws millions of visitors each year. Communal recitation of the rosary and rosary walks continue to be two of the most ardent devotions embraced by pilgrims who visit Lourdes.

Mary Today

The basic time line of Mary's life and her role in church history helped me draw a much clearer picture of Mary as a mother, faithful apostle, pure intercessor, and queen. It was also helpful for me to examine in a practical way her role in the lives of other Catholics around me. All the scholarship in the world cannot account for the gentle, irresistible, personal influence that she has on millions of people, including some of my neighbors, family members, and friends. Few of them had read papal encyclicals or anything on the early church's history, but their everyday devotion had given them a more profound understanding of Mary and her role than anything I had gained through study.

I joined an informal rosary group largely made up of people under thirty who said the rosary every day after noon Mass. The group was often led by a gentle Nigerian man named Kenneth. I first noticed him in church because he received the Eucharist on his knees. It was clear that he did this out of great love and reverence and in no way for show. Kenneth's piety had a profound effect on everyone who knew him. Praying the rosary was truly a transcendental experience for him. When he prayed, his entire demeanor exuded total humility, piety, and tenderness. He would linger on each word of each prayer as if it was the most beautiful and meaningful word ever uttered. He shared his meditations with the rest of us; they were profound, lengthy, and took on an almost mystical quality.

Kenneth was equally generous with his intercession. While I focused much of my prayerful attention on myself, Kenneth always remembered his family, the clergy, the poor, the sick, the suffering, the lonely, the forgotten, and everyone in the group. He was known throughout the community as someone you could call on for any kind of help. The only intention he ever offered for himself was for the ability to accept the will of God for his life. He always seemed engulfed in absolute peace. But what struck me the most was Kenneth's obvious affection for Mary and the depth of his relationship with her.

"Our Blessed Mother was fully human," he said, "so it helps me to identify with her. I also want to emulate her response to God's call in the Annunciation. Even without fully understanding the end she just said yes. That helps me to accept the commandments. Period. My message may be different. Mary received her message through the angel, but I receive my message through the church, through the commandments, through the Scriptures. When I meditate on that mystery, it helps me to say yes to God's will, even though I don't know the details."

Kenneth often described Mary's virtues—her patience, tenderness, motherly attributes, and fortitude. "Even when we begin slacking," he said, "she will continue to pray for us."

Having left his own biological mother in Nigeria, Kenneth said that he related to Mary much as a son would to his mother.

"You know how you would run to your mom for comfort, advice, and all of that?" he asked. "It's disarming when someone accepts you for what you are, no matter how bad you are, no matter what you are. You can't help but trust in her and go to her—especially if she proves to you over and over that she is there for you."

He related many stories of Mary's intervention in his life, not the least of which was the restoration of sight to his right eye. He'd been blind in that eye for almost two decades, but his sight was restored through corneal implant surgery. He attributed both the surgery and the restoration of his sight to rosary devotion and Mary's intercession.

"She is persistent," he said. "When I had given up and believed it when the doctors told me there was no hope, her prayers kept going up for me."

In time I experienced answers to my own prayer, shifts in my attitude and behavior, the softening of character defects that had previously debilitated me, and a greater love for God, myself, and others. I can directly attribute all of this to rosary meditation. As Mother Teresa said, "Our Lady of Cana only thought of the needs of others and made their needs known to Christ." It became clear to me that while Mary acts as our sponsor, our patron, she also prays for us as a parent would pray for his or her own child. Because she holds an honored position as Jesus' mother and an honored place in heaven, it makes sense that we would honor and wish to emulate her example while asking her to join us in presenting our petitions to God.

In *Walking on Water: Reflections on Faith & Art,* Madeleine L'Engle writes, "We do not draw people to Christ by loudly discrediting what they believe, by telling them how wrong they are and how right we are, but by showing them a light that is so lovely that they want with all their hearts to know the source of it." That is the role of Mary, the morning star, to silently shine with such loveliness that we cannot help but want, like the angels, to visit her too.

"Even without fully understanding the end, Mary just said yes. When I meditate on that mystery, it helps me to say yes to God's will, even though I don't know the details."

Kenneth, Nigerian-born nurse

A Path into Prayer

She followed the track, swaying through the quiet bare fields, through the little strings of trees silver in their dead leaves, past cabins silver from weather . . . all like old women under a spell sitting there.
—Eudora Welty, from "A Worn Path"

In Eudora Welty's short story "A Worn Path," Phoenix Jackson, a very poor, very old, southern black woman, is making a trip into town to get medicine for her sick grandson. The boy has been sick for years, and during that time she has often walked this path on his behalf. The story recounts her trials and joys along this sometimes arduous route. She encounters animals, takes a nap under a tree, and later exchanges a few words with a hunter who is walking through the woods with his dog. She experiences a number of small victories and scares along the way. It is, as Welty articulates so beautifully, the story of "the deep-grained habit of love."

But in the end, once Phoenix Jackson has reached the doctor's office, readers discover that her grandson may already be dead and that Phoenix may have made this long trek for naught. No matter—she would have made the journey anyway, out of love for the child. The point of the journey became the journey itself. And so the story takes on another level of meaning. What seems to be the simple chronicle of a woman walking to town is actually a picture of devotion. With every trip, each hardly differing from the last, Phoenix Jackson digs one layer deeper into this path of devotion. It is not the act of walking that becomes the focal point of the story but the path of love that is left behind. The story's final image is of Phoenix, weary and wondering, starting back down the path toward home.

Much the same might be said of rosary devotion. On the surface the rosary resembles Phoenix Jackson's weary path— some simple prayers, a lot of repetition, and a few beads thrown in for easy tracking. But the rosary, like Phoenix's path, is much more than that. Over time, it takes on a transcendent quality; it has the potential to be a very deep prayer, operating on many levels, engaging our bodies, minds, emotions, and spirits. And its practice becomes nothing less than "the deep-grained habit of love."

The rosary is a physical object that has developed over time, but it mirrors God and his creation in a remarkable way. It is circular, implying a never-ending nature. Within this nature is a sense of wholeness, security, and purpose, a sense of moving forward in and deeper into our love for and devotion to God. Like nature's seasons, the rosary is cyclical and perfectly balanced: one part joy, one part light, one part sorrow, one part glory. It meets us in every circumstance. Despite its simplicity, it works in ways we cannot fully understand. Its order and balance draw us into deeper meditation and open us to contemplation, which is a deep experience of God's presence or, as Quaker author Richard Foster puts it, "the silence of God."

"I love to go to the beach and walk there at night. I love the sound of waves coming in. The rosary, in some regards, is a bit like that. It's like those waves coming in that form a repetitious pattern that allows a person to more deeply meditate."

Fr. Eric Fowlkes, parish priest

Each decade of Hail Marys inevitably leads us back to the Our Father—the prayer Christ taught us himself. And so Mary leads us to the Father—the source of all life, all grace—again and again. With him we linger for a while, contemplating the next mystery, recalling our petition or thanksgiving, asking once again for the Lord to be present to us in our meditation, praying his perfect prayer.

The rhythm and balance and order in the rosary contribute to its meditative effect. We need only begin. Once we get the hang of this simple little prayer, we can pray it in the car, on subways, and in taxis; standing in line at the grocery store or waiting in the doctor's office; walking to school or walking the dog; in groups or alone; with our families or with tapes; as petition, as preparation, as praise; in reparation or in thanksgiving. The deep meditation we tap into in solitary rosary devotion will visit us again wherever we pray the rosary. Many rosary devotees claim that the peace their prayer brings lingers with them long after they've finished praying.

The Attitude of Prayer

Praying is a human activity common to all peoples. It has existed since the beginning of human history and is found in some form in every race, creed, culture, and civilization. It is not reserved for "religious" people only. Anyone can pray; it involves simply speaking to God, either vocally or mentally. St. Thérèse of Lisieux said that prayer "is a surge of the heart; it is a simple look turned toward heaven." Another definition offered by St. John Damascene is "Prayer is the raising of one's mind and heart to God." Praying involves directing your thoughts and affections toward God. We are encouraged often throughout Scripture "to pray always and not to lose heart" (Luke 18:1). Prayer is a conversation with God that we can be involved in constantly, throughout our day and during all our activities.

I think of prayer as my pathway to God. Like Phoenix Jackson, I'm on a journey for medicine, only the medicine I seek is of a spiritual nature. Like that old woman, I sometimes walk the path for the sake of others. Sometimes I walk for myself. Sometimes I walk just for love of the path itself—the places it takes me and the adventures and sites I encounter along the way. Sometimes I'm on the path for no particular reason at all. In fact, I've come to see that I'm really on the path all the time.

It's an expedition of ever-deepening trust. Thomas Keating, a Cistercian monk and the founder of the centering-prayer movement, wrote, "The Christian spiritual path is based on a deepening trust in God. It is trust that first allows us to take that initial leap in the dark, to encounter God at deeper levels of ourselves. And it is trust that guides the intimate refashioning of our being, the transformation of our pain, woundedness, and unconscious motivation into the person that God intended us to be." When we talk with a friend, we are shaped by our conversation; it becomes a part of us. Prayer—conversation with God—has the same effect. It results in a transformation of the one praying. You. Me. That is a scary business. We typically pray in hopes that our circumstances will change, only to discover that it's we who need to change. If you feel trepidation at the start of your journey of prayer, take comfort in the fact that many have gone before you and know the way—by heart.

Because it's simple, rosary meditation can be a good way to begin to build the trust that all prayer requires. For example, in my greatest time of distress, the rosary asked very little of me, which helped set the stage for the process of building trust. Building trust requires time and attention, and a habit of praying the rosary regularly allows you to build that trust, one step at a time, one decade at a time. Like any journey, prayer begins right where you are and proceeds step-by-step. If you're in Beijing and you want to get to Paris, you start in Beijing, not New York. The road may seem long, but with steady progress and a trusting heart you may find yourself eating truffles while staring at the Eiffel Tower before you know it. What's more, you might get to your destination by an entirely different route than the one you had initially mapped for yourself. Prayer is a path full of surprises.

After years of walking the path of prayer, you will likely find that much has changed. Your fear of connecting with God will have left you. Prayer will have become as natural as breathing. The time you allot for prayer and meditation will be a time you look forward to with great, peaceful anticipation instead of apprehension or reluctance. You will go to prayer like a carefree child. Some days will certainly present more obstacles than others. Some days the path will be all uphill. Other days you'll be distracted by slippery slopes or wild animals hidden in the bushes. But you will pass through these obstacles as safely as Phoenix Jackson did and will start back down the path again, the path toward your spiritual home.

Pope John Paul II's Love for the Rosary

Karol Wojtyla discovered Marian devotion at a time when circumstances threatened Catholic lives. His native country of Poland was under Nazi occupation as World War II raged in Europe. He was a young man, working in a factory and trying not to attract the attention of the German authorities. During the occupation, workers like Wojtyla might leave for the factory in the morning and simply never return. Daily life during the war was cruelly uncertain.

The rosary and other Marian devotions had long been popular in Poland. Wojtyla had shied away from Marian devotion as a young man, thinking that he needed to focus more on Christ. But as his rosary devotion grew, he came to realize that the rosary was profoundly Christocentric. This realization was a great comfort to him and deepened his prayer life immeasurably.

When he wasn't working in the factory, Wojtyla studied literature and had ambitions to become an actor. During the occupation, he and his friends gathered for what they called "rhapsodic theater," "the artistic recitation of poetry." They wanted to "regenerate the world by a display of artistic beauty." He was also strongly drawn to theology and philology. He read deeply in the works of the great mystics, especially St. John of the Cross and St. Teresa of Ávila. His prayer life, which had always been important to him, intensified through the inspiration of such contemplatives.

Central to his prayer life throughout this period was rosary meditation. He and fourteen other young men formed a Living Rosary group despite the fact that these meetings might get them shipped off to concentration camps or shot. The Nazis had banned studies for the priesthood as part of their attempt to crush the church in Poland. But Wojtyla defied the ban. He was admitted into seminary studies that took place in secret and was ordained in 1946.

Wojtyla's prayer life, formed under such threatening circumstances, remains an inspiration to the world as he heads the church as Pope John Paul II. Since the earliest days of his papacy, Pope John Paul II has strongly advocated Marian devotion and rosary meditation in particular. In his Angelus message from October 29, 1978, just thirteen days after he became pope, he summed up the rosary in this way:

The rosary is my favorite prayer. A marvelous prayer! Marvelous in its simplicity and in its depth. In this prayer we repeat many times the words that the Virgin Mary heard from the Archangel, and from her kinswoman Elizabeth. The whole Church joins in these words. It can be said that the rosary is, in a certain way, a prayer-commentary on . . . the wonderful presence of the Mother of God in the mystery of Christ and the Church.

In fact, against the background of the words "Ave Maria" there pass before the eyes of the soul the main episodes in the life of Jesus Christ. They are composed altogether in the joyful, sorrowful, and glorious mysteries, and they put us in living communion with Jesus through—we could say—his Mother's heart.

At the same time our heart can enclose in these decades of the rosary all the facts that make up the life of the individual, the family, the nation, the Church, and mankind. Personal matters and those of one's neighbor, and particularly of those who are closest to us, who are dearest to us. Thus the simple prayer of the rosary beats the rhythm of human life.

His devotion to Mary and to the rosary has deepened throughout his twenty-five-year papacy. In his apostolic letter of October 2002, Rosarium Virginis Mariae, the Pope writes,

To pray the Rosary is to hand over our burdens to the merciful hearts of Christ and his Mother. Twenty-five years later, thinking back over the difficulties which have also been part of my exercise

of the Petrine ministry, I feel the need to say once more, as a warm invitation to everyone to experience it personally: the Rosary does indeed "mark the rhythm of human life", bringing it into harmony with the "rhythm" of God's own life, in the joyful communion of the Holy Trinity, our life's destiny and deepest longing.

The letter goes on to declare the year 2003 the Year of the Rosary and publicly endorses the addition of the luminous mysteries to the traditional joyful, sorrowful, and glorious mysteries, further enhancing our understanding of the rosary as a living prayer, evolving and growing along with the faithful who practice its meditations. Capturing the public ministry of Jesus, the luminous mysteries provide rich opportunities for deeper reflection on the meaning of baptism, the Eucharist, evangelization, leadership, adoration, and the power of Christ's friendship to restore and transform us.

Calling on the church to become "distinguished above all in the art of prayer," the pope writes,

It is during the years of his public ministry that the mystery of Christ is most evidently a mystery of light: "While I am in the world, I am the light of the world." This addition of these new mysteries, without prejudice to any essential aspect of the prayer's traditional format, is meant to give it fresh life and to enkindle renewed interest in the Rosary's place within Christian spirituality as a true doorway to the depths of the Heart of Christ, ocean of joy and of light, of suffering and of glory.

The Act of Prayer

No amount of study or intellectualizing can replace the actual practice of rosary meditation. Just as a writer must eventually stop planning and start writing, the person who plans to pray must eventually start to pray. You cannot think your way into rosary devotion. At some point, you must pick up the beads and take action.

But the act of praying is a blessed act. As St. Paul tells us, "the Spirit helps us in our weakness; for we do not know how to pray as we ought, but that very Spirit intercedes with sighs too deep for words" (Romans 8:26). In rosary devotion, we ask Mary to intercede for us. Through the same Holy Spirit that overshadowed her, she joins in our prayers with unique fervor.

The rosary addresses some of the common problems we have with prayer. It gives us a common language, which conversation and communication require. Perhaps when you enter into God's presence you are shy and tongue-tied—an understandable reaction to meeting someone for the first time. Or perhaps you have an unrealistically exalted notion of how sophisticated prayer needs to be. Because of its uniformity, the rosary is an excellent prayer for overcoming such obstacles. The rosary can be prayed easily with groups or alone with little worry about "What will I say?" As Pope Pius XI wrote, the rosary is "without doubt easy for all." In a way, the rosary does the work for you. To do it, you only need to show up.

People pray the rosary in many different ways—formally and informally, in solitude and with company, with varying degrees of meditation. Many people like to say the rosary in groups. This is especially true of older Catholics, many of whom probably prayed the rosary more often in communal settings. Joining a rosary group may help those who are just starting a rosary devotion to familiarize themselves with it. Your local Catholic church should be able to point you in the direction of a Legion of Mary group or some other group that practices a rosary devotion. Other people prefer to pray the rosary alone. This seems to be especially true of young people, who seem to have a greater need to meditate in order to handle the chaos of modern life.

You may wish to give some thought to *where* you pray the rosary. Most people like a quiet place—a room or a park where they won't be disturbed. Churches are an obvious choice. Many people focus on the visual cues found in churches—a crucifix, a statue of the Madonna, the tabernacle, and other holy objects. Many devotees find kneeling to be the best posture for prayer, and it is easy to find a comfortable place to kneel in most churches. Other people pray the rosary while moving around. The steady rhythm of walking, running, or even riding a bike helps them to enter into deeper meditation. Many people pray the rosary while waiting in traffic or sitting in buses or on airplanes. One woman I know keeps track of how far it is to various destinations by the number of decades of the rosary she can say during her trip.

Many people find it helpful to begin their rosary meditation with an Act of Contrition and a prayer to the Holy Spirit. If you are Catholic, make regular use of the sacraments, including confession. If regular confession is not an option or if you are not Catholic, it may be useful to write out a confession of sorts—a list of problems or questions that you would like to bring to the attention of Christ with the help of the Blessed Mother. Read them aloud before you begin; make your first prayer "I'm not sure what I'm doing here, please help me." No special eloquence is required; the simplest prayers are often the best.

Rarely do I pray without a pen and notebook nearby. A copious diarist since childhood, I record my answers to prayer along with the insights and ideas that come to me while meditating. I pray most often for direction from God. Inevitably, he offers it. Solutions to problems will present themselves as I pray the rosary, and I find it helpful to write them down as they arrive. It has also been valuable for me to look back over years of prayer and see how my meditation and devotion have developed. However, some people find writing distracting to their meditation. Others journal for a few moments before or after their meditation to gently "clear the mental decks." Others track nothing at all on paper. You will soon discover what methods enhance your communion with God.

Distractions may make deep prayer difficult, but prayer does not necessarily need to be exceedingly deep to be deeply effective. I've learned not to fight my distractions but to lean into them, to embrace them. Sometimes I may stop my prayer and name the distraction: "Lord, I'm distracted by the people talking behind me as I'm trying to pray. Please help me get quiet inside myself." Or, "Lord, I can't get my workload out of my mind. Help me to be present to you." Surprisingly, those very distractions are often the means by which God leads me to a new understanding, an insight or an answer to a problem. God uses *everything* to get our attention. Don't assume that because you are distracted you are doing something wrong. That you are aware of your distractions is probably an indication that you are on the right track.

Beginning Rosary Meditation

Once you've presented your confession and petitions to God, begin the rosary with the sign of the cross. Some people hold the crucifix in their right hand when they make the sign of the cross, kissing it on completion. I am fond of this tradition for three reasons: one, I am an affectionate person and I appreciate appropriate public displays of affection, especially toward God; two, physical actions attached to the devotion help to make it more visceral for me and deepen the entire experience; and three, I am then poised for the first prayer.

On the crucifix, say the Apostles' Creed. The creed is essentially a "list" prayer of the tenets of the faith, almost a litany. Lists based on theology may be overwhelming for first-time meditators, but I have found that when I slow this prayer down, it takes on a whole new character: it is not a long and lofty list that I must wade through, but a true declaration of my faith that allows me to join all the angels and saints in heaven who live this declaration for eternity. I frequently take one tenet of the creed each time I pray the rosary and spend an extra moment reflecting on it. For example, I might repeat several times, "I believe in the resurrection of the body." I will reflect on what that means exactly—that Christ died and after three days rose from the dead and walked around and talked with people. Because the tenets of the creed and the mysteries overlap and reflect one another, reflecting on the tenets one by one also helps to deepen my meditations on the mysteries.

On the first bead, say an Our Father. Of all the prayers in the rosary, this is the most difficult prayer for me to say because it requires the most of me—a submission, a turning over of my will to God's. It requires trust. The Lord's Prayer is the beginning of the recognition process, of seeing God as my true Father and as one who is trustworthy. If you're having trouble saying the Our Father, you might want to concentrate on the first portion of the prayer. Get a notebook and write out your present relationship to the heavenly Father (not your earthly father, unless that helps remind you of qualities that your heavenly Father possesses). You may want to reflect on some of the following Scriptures and what they tell us about the nature of our heavenly Father:

- "Cast all your anxiety on him, because he cares for you" (1 Peter 5:7). The Father loves you and is interested in you.

- "Do not be afraid, little flock, for it is your Father's good pleasure to give you the kingdom" (Luke 12:32). He delights in giving you good things.

- "I will be your father, and you shall be my sons and daughters" (2 Corinthians 6:18). He wants to be with you; he has claimed you as his own.

- "You open your hand, satisfying the desire of every living thing" (Psalm 145:16). He provides. He satisfies.

- "He heals the brokenhearted, and binds up their wounds" (Psalm 147:3). He heals and comforts.

- "Father of orphans and protector of widows is God in his holy habitation" (Psalm 68:5). Our heavenly Father can help us overcome any fatherlessness we may feel.

Ask God to reveal to you the ways in which he has been a father to you. What has he done for you that you might praise him for? Has he given you the gift of life? a friend who loves you? a good brain? Has he given you the ability to read this book? to ask questions? to wonder and imagine? Perhaps you can recognize the Father's hand in creation around you, in the beauty of the earth, the oceans, or animals. It is important to be open to seeing the Father's active presence in your life. God is not up in heaven waiting for you to "get it right" before he will join in a conversation with you. As Thomas Merton, addressing the Father, wrote, "You do not wait for me to become great before you will be with me and hear me and answer me." You can be confident that no matter how weak or unskilled your efforts in prayer might be right now, God hears you and is interested in what you have to say.

Parts of the Lord's Prayer might give you difficulty. Maybe you don't mean it when you say, "thy will be done" or "we forgive those who trespass against us." Those are very powerful words. But to say "thy will be done" or "we forgive," even if we don't entirely mean that at the time, is a step in the right direction toward actually meaning it. If nothing else, it demonstrates to God our willingness to learn to forgive as he has forgiven us and to learn to bend to his will. Our emotions on the matter will eventually catch up with our actions.

On each of the next three beads, say the Hail Mary, dedicating one to the virtue of faith, one to hope, and one to charity. Ask Mary to please pray for you so that you may live out those virtues more fully. With each Hail Mary, you are positioning yourself to accept, as Mary did, God's will for your life. You are sharing in the Incarnation, the Word made flesh. Jesus is central to the Hail Mary. The words of the angel Gabriel as well as the inspired words of Elizabeth celebrate the most longed-for moment in history. When we recall these words, we participate in this moment. We share—acutely, personally—the longing in Mary's own heart for the Messiah; we join in her obedience, her "yes," which ultimately allowed for salvation. In doing so, we too participate in the work of salvation. In many ways, the rosary is a reminder not only to strive for the virtues described and celebrated within its mysteries but also to model ourselves after the specifically evangelical example of Mary. When I say a Hail Mary I am simply asking someone I trust and admire, someone I believe led a holy, virtuous life, to please pray for me. I need all the righteous prayers I can get.

After the three Hail Marys, say the doxology, recognizing God's eternal character and thanking him for letting you be a part of eternity. Like Mary, like all of us, you have an eternal role to play in the "world without end."

After the doxology, move on to the next bead, where you will begin the first decade by meditating on the first mystery and saying an Our Father. At this point, some people simply announce the mystery and then recall in their minds the events of that mystery while praying the decade. For example, if the mystery is the Crucifixion, they might recall Christ stretched out on the cross, the nails in his hands and feet, the wound at his side, and the crown of thorns. They might also bring to mind the Blessed Mother in agony as she watched her child suffer. In chapters 6 through 9, which focus on the mysteries of the rosary, a Scripture passage and a prayer are provided to help you visualize each mystery more vividly.

Before each decade, or group of ten Hail Marys, meditate on a mystery. As you pray, keep your mind and heart open to receive anything that the Lord would like to tell you, any insight he would like to share with you. If you have trouble concentrating on the mysteries, you may wish to add after each Hail Mary a reference to the mystery being contemplated. Conclude each decade with the doxology. Continue this cycle throughout the rest of the mysteries.

Remember that it's not necessary (and may not even be possible) to pray the rosary *perfectly*. Many of the saints seated in heaven right now struggled to pray the rosary. Meditation, regardless of its form, takes time and practice. When I first started, I wasn't able to remember some of the mysteries, much less recount them in order or meditate on them thoughtfully. I had to borrow a rosary that had the mysteries written on elongated Our Father beads so that I could remember which mystery was to be recited on which day. Some people find it helpful to refer to a notecard that has the prayers and the mysteries written on it.

The point is to simply begin and begin simply. If one mystery in particular really draws you, start there. You may discover that you prefer to say one decade when you first get up, one or two at lunchtime, and the rest in the evening before bed. Or maybe one decade a day is all you can manage. The amount you can pray is not nearly as important as the attitude you bring to your prayer. Be open. Don't try to begin in New York if you're in Beijing. Your efforts will be well rewarded and well guided.

A New Citizen

Family rosary meditation was a part of Kenneth's devout Catholic upbringing in Nigeria. Yet when Kenneth was a teenager he abandoned his spiritual life, as many young people do. The bad grades he received in college and the declining state of Nigeria left him feeling hopeless for any kind of future. In desperation, he returned to the rosary for answers.

"When I first started with the rosary again it was ritual, routine. I just said it," says Kenneth. "I struggled to complete the five decades. I just prayed it. I would forget the mysteries and have to check with a book. I was just trying to get the hang of it, the rhythm of praying the rosary.

"It was a confusing time," he continues. "God was so big. I didn't know how to approach him for help. Praying the rosary helped. When I had questions, I prayed the rosary, and Mary provided answers one way or the other. In time, I realized that she was supplying answers to my questions. But still, God was so big, big, big. I would attend Mass, but it didn't really mean that much internally; I still didn't have faith. But Mary was successful in drawing me closer to it, to helping me understand it. . . . She has been very helpful, like a true mother walking with her child step-by-step, but it's only been afterward that I've realized how she has helped me."

Kenneth says that there were many times on his spiritual path when he questioned doctrines of the church, and during those times of questioning he "would be inspired to go back to the rosary. . . . Praying the rosary, gradually the understanding would come. It has a way of taking such a lofty doctrine, mysteries, and applying them to our level. . . . In his divine nature, no matter how simple he makes himself, we will still not comprehend God, so he has given us the rosary to simplify some things."

Kenneth credits the rosary with transforming his temperament from hotheaded to calm, quiet, and supportive.

"In reflection on the mysteries I came to see that we are called to be like Christ and we are to leave our old self aside and to put on the new self."

Kenneth experienced many extraordinary answers to prayer through his rosary devotion, but probably the most dramatic occurred when he decided to try to come to the United States. At the time, his native Nigeria was in turmoil (and unfortunately still is). The economy was suffering and crime was at an all-time high. "The future was dark," he says, "just nothing." He wanted to come to the United States, but he knew that obtaining a visa to leave was next to impossible, especially for a young, unmarried man just out of college who might not return to Nigeria if given the chance to leave.

Still, Kenneth had been praying, and despite the fact that he'd applied for a visa before and had been turned down, he believed that the United States was where he was supposed to be.

"I had all the odds against me, so again I just started to pray. The day that I was finally called for an interview I joined a long line at the U.S. embassy. I was there at 5:00 a.m. The building didn't open until nine, but I was there at five just to get a number to get in the building that day. By the time I got there, there were already over two hundred people, so I was praying and praying that they wouldn't cut off the line, because at some point they would. I had heard that people would get called and would not even get in the building. For some reason that day, they just took many more people than they usually did."

Once inside the building, Kenneth was forced to wait again, within earshot of others applying for visas. His tension mounted.

"Every single person I heard that day was rejected," he says. "People would go in there with hope and they would return downcast. I felt terrible. Cold sweat. Shaking. Headache. When it got to about three people before me, I couldn't take it anymore and I left the building. I couldn't concentrate and went outside and started praying the rosary, praying over and over and over. I was just panicked."

Demonstrating emotion of any kind would have been risky. Applicants were often turned down for "emotional problems" if when they arrived at the window their faces revealed any emotion, even joy.

"I said, 'Mother, you have to do this.' All of a sudden I was calm; a certain peace descended on me."

Kenneth went back inside the building. Usually, if you missed your turn, that was it. Instead, he was allowed to walk straight to the first available window.

"They asked me a few questions—where are you going, how long will you be staying, and so on—and then the official looked over my paperwork and said, 'Well, congratulations, welcome to the United States.'

"I waited until I got out of the building, and then I just shouted. What I got that day was a four-year visa. Everybody else got turned down."

Kenneth went on to complete another college degree, this time with high marks, and now practices nursing in the

United States, where he is preparing to become a citizen and enter medical school.

When Your Prayers Seem to Go Unanswered

Volumes have been written on the subject of unanswered prayer and periods of dryness in prayer life, but I only want to briefly discuss these subjects here. Unanswered prayer and dryness in prayer are common experiences. Everyone who practices the spiritual discipline of prayer has struggled with them at some point. Many saints experienced long dry periods during which they were unable to pray or prayed with less than saintly fervor. Even the most pious and saintly people sometimes turn a doubtful glance toward heaven and ask, "Have you been listening to me?" It's likely that at some point you may find yourself asking, "Is this prayer working?"

St. James said, "You ask and do not receive, because you ask wrongly, in order to spend what you get on your pleasures" (James 4:3). Sure, we've all been tempted with prayers like "Please, Lord, let me win the lottery," but what about the times when what we're asking for is completely rational and selfless? We pray for our sick loved ones to be healed, yet they remain ill or even get worse; we pray for work so that we can support our family, yet we continue to struggle financially; we pray for companionship, a spouse or friend, and yet each day we wake up alone and lonely. Sometimes the answer to our prayer is no and sometimes it's "not yet." Other times, God is waiting to teach us something or offer us something better than we ever expected, if only we can remain open to receiving it.

Take the example of twenty-eight-year-old Carl, a systems analyst who has been praying the rosary for five years.

"The rosary provides me with so many opportunities to connect with God," he said. "There's the physical part, moving the beads through the fingers; the vocal prayer; and then the mental, meditative reflecting on the scene—there are so many different levels of activity. The rosary fulfills St. Paul's command that we 'pray without ceasing.' It has forced me to see virtues that I need. I need humility. I'm not proud of that, no pun intended. If I weren't praying the rosary, I don't think in the normal course of prayer that humility would strike me as something that I needed to pray for. The same is true for all of the mysteries. It wouldn't have occurred to me that faith is something that I need to ask for, that it's a gift."

In his meditation, Carl has found that his attitude toward life in general has begun to shift. He is less drawn to material things and more to eternal activities. He has come to believe that God has called all Christians not to hide away from the world, but to "get into the fabric of life" in order to effect change. Rosary meditation has changed Carl, especially through his "unanswered" prayer.

"Praying the rosary," he said, "has made it easier for me to accept the will of God. When I finished the MBA program, I was ready to leave my job, and I applied for this one particular job and I was praying for it, saying, 'Okay, dear God, I'm asking you for this job, I really want it.' I prayed and I prayed, I offered all my rosaries for that intention, but I would also say, 'If it's not your will for me to have it, then that's okay, but did I tell you I *really* want it?' Then, after all of that, I didn't get the job."

He was disappointed and downtrodden, but he continued to pray, asking God to help him accept his circumstances. Nine months later he got a promotion. In every way his new position was better than the job he'd prayed for so diligently.

Years into his devotion, Carl said, "I have had very few prayers, if any, that have gone unanswered."

The prayer that seems to go unanswered may be an opportunity for your faith to grow, for you to learn daily persistence in the spiritual discipline of meditation.

Prayer is an extraordinary gift that God has reserved for his most precious creation—human beings. In rosary meditation, we are reminded that he is our Father and that he longs for our attention, affection, and interest. He promises that he will walk beside us along this path of transformation, guiding us and teaching us to pray, not only through the Lord's Prayer but also through the example of the Blessed Mother.

When the disciples beckoned, "Lord, teach us to pray," what they really desired was to find God, to discover the path that might take them into his presence. They wanted that childlike connection. What they learned, and what we are still learning through the rosary, is that the discovery of this path is only the beginning. We need to tread it thoughtfully, often, and with a certain spontaneity and willingness to accept the places it takes us.

"After praying the rosary for some time, I've found myself really turned away from and turned off by materialism. [The rosary] seems to have opened my eyes to an entirely new world: one where spiritual matters are so much more important and more interesting than physical things."

Jennifer, a new mother

The Rosary as Meditation

Through the study of books one seeks God; by meditation one finds him.
—Padre Pio

The rosary is a powerful spiritual tool for meditation. While meditation grows in popularity as a means to better mental, physical, and spiritual health, many people, including many Catholics, overlook the rosary as a meditative tool. It is sometimes seen as too simple and therefore as superficial. The rosary is simple, but the gentle repetition of its prayers makes it an excellent means to moving into deeper meditation. It gives us an opportunity to open ourselves to God's word, to refine our interior gaze by turning our minds to the life of Christ.

By focusing on the lives of Christ and Mary through meditation on the mysteries, we learn about ourselves in relation to God. Mary herself is an excellent model for the daily practice of meditation. She received the word of God through Gabriel. She pondered God's word in her heart. She took in the events around her, capturing them internally and carrying them within her like a treasure. This is the essence of meditation—receiving God's word and making it our treasure.

And our choice. As Richard Foster notes, "in meditative prayer God is always addressing our will. Christ confronts us and asks us to choose. Having heard his voice . . . we are called to life-transforming obedience." Meditation gives us the option to be transformed. We must choose it.

You may have objections. "I'm not a monk living in seclusion. I don't know a thing about meditation. How can someone like me meditate?" But meditation is for all believers, not just for monks like Thomas Merton. As Merton himself reminds us, "We must not imagine the early monks applying themselves to a very intellectual and analytical 'meditation' of the Bible. Meditation for them consisted in making the words of the Bible their own by memorizing them and repeating them, with deep and simple concentration." We don't have to make meditation complicated to make it meaningful. The rosary contains the necessary elements for simple meditation. Praying it with "deep and simple concentration," recalling the events of the mysteries and pausing to think about them for a moment, can draw us into a deeper relationship with God—the goal of meditation.

Indeed, many people use the rosary in precisely this way.

Francesco, a college student preparing for the priesthood, uses the rosary in a variety of ways, but particularly as a means to meditate. Rosary devotion was passed down in his family from his mother, and her simple meditations gave him greater insight into his faith and his relationship with God.

"As a kid, I would always turn to the rosary as something to pray," he said. "It was a very Catholic thing to do that we did in our house all the time. It's very simple, but when you pray it, you feel close to God."

It was from this simple, childlike relationship with the rosary that Francesco's meditations matured.

"Every time I visit the meditations they get deeper and deeper and deeper," he said. "You grow in the meditations."

Francesco's own meditations are not necessarily cerebral or complicated, but they are rich and deeply felt.

"The agony in the garden is a very powerful meditation, where you experience how the agony must have been almost more agonizing than the Crucifixion itself. The anticipation made the Crucifixion more agonizing because Christ had a choice to make. It helps you with the different choices you have to make. The rosary is a very, very deep prayer. It's complex because the situation is beyond words, the things God does for us are beyond words."

Francesco grew up with a passionate love for the rosary, and he seems to have a gift for meditation. That is not the case with everyone. It is not the case with me. Meditation did not come easily for me, nor does it still. I think that my experience of struggling with rosary meditation is perhaps the more common experience. I have had to learn about meditation and have had to practice it diligently.

How to Meditate

Thomas Merton wrote that "meditation is really very simple and there is not much need of elaborate techniques to teach us how to go about it." Nevertheless, Merton wrote prolifically on the subject. We can begin to understand meditation by learning about the basic principles that govern it.

The first principle is that meditation is learned through practice. Like Francesco, many people who practice rosary meditation begin very simply and gradually develop a more sophisticated meditation. The meditator learns to hear an interior voice, the voice of God. The church calls meditation a "quest." It is an experience of prayer that reaches beyond the experience itself to something deeper. In the *Catechism,* the church teaches that "Christian prayer should go further: to the knowledge of the love of the Lord Jesus, to union with him." This takes time, and it demands that the one who is praying focus on God's love for us, a love he demonstrates through union with Christ.

Solitude and a routine can greatly assist meditation. Find a quiet, private room where you can light a candle or play soft music. Many people find it helpful to set aside a specific time each day for meditation. Enter your meditation dates into your calendar or put a note on the refrigerator: "Meditation for ten minutes at 3:00 p.m." Fight the urge to feel guilty about taking time for something as "useless" or as "silly" as meditation might feel at first. Start simply. I suggest that you begin any meditation with a prayer to the Holy Spirit asking for guidance and for freedom from distractions.

Once you've selected your posture and created an environment that is fit for meditation, close your eyes and take a few deep, slow breaths. Try to relax your body; become aware of your breathing. Then begin the rosary. As distractions or problems come to mind, simply acknowledge them and move on. If you are plagued by thoughts of problems or of people, invite them to "have a seat" while you pray. They can sit there while you continue to meditate. Don't struggle to rid your mind of all distractions or to force every troubling thought out of your head. Acknowledge these distractions and bring them to God.

Gently focus on each mystery as you reach it in the course of praying the rosary. You might find it helpful to read some devotional material about the mystery, such as the reflections in the following chapters. You might also listen to music, write, or practice exercises of the imagination.

Because the traditional mysteries are so visually oriented, I will sometimes begin my meditation by painting the scene in my imagination. For example, I might think about what kind of a brush and what colors I would use for the nativity of Jesus. I would think about painting the picture, about how I would depict the gentleness and innocence of a newborn. As I would begin to work on the picture in my mind, my meditation might settle on the virtues of gentleness and innocence. Where in my life is Jesus teaching me how to be gentle, tender? Where in my life can I model the innocence of a newborn child? In what area of my life do I need to place my total trust in Jesus, relying on him for my every need, or to become more childlike and less childish?

Many people find music helpful in rosary meditation. If you are especially moved by music, find a favorite piece of music that lends itself to joyfulness, luminosity, sorrow, or glory, depending on the mysteries you are praying. Choose a hymn to accompany each mystery or choose lyrics that call to mind the scene of the mystery. Several people I know pray the rosary with the help of the "Ave Maria" and other Marian songs.

If your imagination is stirred more by words than by images, write out a description of the scene of the mystery or read the full Scripture passage describing it. These passages are printed in the following chapters. Read them, and choose a verse that particularly strikes you.

For example, I read this verse while praying the mystery of the Nativity: "And she gave birth to her firstborn son and wrapped him in bands of cloth, and laid him in a manger, because there was no place for them in the inn" (Luke 2:7). I was struck by the phrase "she gave birth." I realized that to give birth means to give to the world what was exclusively yours for nine months. Preparation is over; it's now time to give away. I asked myself if I am being called to give something away, not physically like Mary, but creatively. How am I offering my creativity, my imagination, my self, my gifts to God?

Meditation proceeds in this way. It means reflecting on the words or images that each mystery brings to mind and remaining open to what God would have us understand about how those events relate to our lives.

Don't try to force meditation, and don't make it complicated. Simplify it. Rosary meditation has shown me that some
of the greatest soul-stirring moments take place in the gentle,
ordinary events of everyday life. Mary had an everyday life—in
her simple, humble ways, she had a child, cared for him, and
was a mother and wife. I have an everyday life—I get up each
day, write out my morning pages, go to Mass, pay bills or clean
house, say the rosary, and go on about my day. It is in these
simple, ordinary things of life that meditation finds the great
spiritual drama.

"Love the Madonna and Pray the Rosary"

Padre Pio (1887–1968), an Italian Capuchin monk, is one of
the most beloved saints of modern times. Many supernatural
events are associated with him, including the stigmata, or the
wounds of Christ, which he received in 1918. He was a
beloved confessor and friend to thousands. He said that
those who requested his prayers in a sincere attitude of piety
and humility were his "spiritual children"—he believed that
before he died he would have a spiritual family that would
span the entire globe.

Padre Pio was deeply devoted to the Blessed Mother and
the rosary. Those close to him said that he prayed the rosary
as many as thirty-five times a day. Pictures of Padre Pio often
show him with his hand in his upper-right chest-pocket,
where it was believed he kept up an almost constant devotion,

praying the rosary while he carried on with other tasks throughout the day. A recording of him saying the rosary was even broadcast over the radio. Greatly enamored of our Lady, he said, "Love the Madonna and pray the rosary, for her rosary is the weapon against the evils of the world today."

Padre Pio was devoted in particular to the practice of meditation, which is probably one of the reasons he so favored the rosary. He likened not meditating to going out without looking in the mirror to see if you were clean and neat. He said that "the person who meditates and turns his mind to God, who is the mirror of his soul, seeks to know his faults, tries to correct them, moderates his impulses, and puts his conscience in order."

He called prayer "the best armor we have . . . the key which opens the heart of God." He encouraged those who practiced meditation to "have patience in the perseverance of the holy exercise" and to "be content to begin by making little steps until you have legs to run with, or rather, wings to fly with."

Padre Pio (who was canonized on September 23, 2000) died on September 23, 1968, with his rosary beads in his hands. More than one hundred thousand people attended his funeral.

Clearing the Interior Space

With time, a key principle of meditation becomes clear: prayer is much more a matter of *being* than of *doing*. Our culture prizes *doing*—tasks and end results. But in prayer we experience *being*—the eternal value of our very souls.

The rosary allows us to profoundly experience being. Indeed, Mary's participation in the Incarnation was not an external accomplishment or an act that only involved her body. It involved her entire being—*body, mind, and soul.* The rosary perfectly engages all three and therefore acts as an ideal means for developing the interior gaze.

The rosary has a rhythm. As with music, in which melody is drawn forward through rhythm, the rosary draws us more deeply into the "melody" of our meditation. Pope Paul VI described it this way: "By its nature the recitation of the rosary calls for a quiet rhythm and a lingering pace, helping the individual to meditate on the mysteries of the Lord's life as seen through the eyes of her who was closest to the Lord. In this way the unfathomable riches of these mysteries are unfolded."

As the mysteries unfold, we cultivate a rich interior life. Usually, we neglect our interior life, which feeds us as beings, because we are preoccupied with fending off the bombardment of external stimuli in our daily lives. Meditation helps to clear the mental, emotional, and spiritual space we need in order to plant our interior vision. It is not a way to avoid chaos or activity, but a means to prepare for it. We do not practice rosary meditation as a means to zone out, but rather to zero in, to concentrate our interior gaze tightly on the Savior and on our need for salvation, conversion, faith, hope, and love.

Some types of meditation foster a lack of activity, an emptying or a stillness of the mind. But rosary meditation is deeply active. Unlike some Eastern meditation practices that ask the meditator to detach from everything and cultivate nothingness, rosary meditation asks us to attach ourselves to the virtues that each mystery celebrates and to allow ourselves to be filled with God's love, grace, and wisdom.

The Rhythm of the Rosary

Fr. Eric Fowlkes, a parish priest in rural Tennessee, converted to Catholicism when he was sixteen. The rosary acted as a catalyst in the process. A Catholic friend from high school taught him how to say it, and after he started praying it he began attending Mass. He felt immediately at home, quickly converted, and soon knew that he was meant to be a priest.

The rhythm of the rosary is important to his meditation. "It provides a rhythm and a pattern and allows the person to enter into a deeper experience of God's presence and of prayer," he says. "I love to go to the beach and walk there at night. I love the sound of waves coming in. The rosary, in some regards, is a bit like that. It's like those waves coming in that form a repetitious pattern that allows a person to more deeply meditate."

Fr. Fowlkes says that the rosary is especially valuable in times of crisis, when praying it may be all we are capable of doing.

"When someone has died, the rosary is particularly powerful," he says. "In times of crisis, we go back to the basics. It's about making connections with very basic things. And I think the rosary helps us connect with a basic trust and faith in God and in the power of intercessory prayer.

"When people are under a lot of pressure, which is about most of us most of the time, I find that the rosary is particularly helpful because it's not complicated. It's a way to have some prayer time without it becoming another burden to add to a long, long list of things."

Meditating on the Mysteries

The chapters that follow offer reflections and prayers to enhance and stimulate meditation on the twenty mysteries of the rosary.

The word *mystery* does not refer to conundrums that can never be solved. Mysteries in this sense are expressions of God's divinity as enacted in the lives of Christ and Mary. Each mystery revolves around virtues. Our purpose in rosary meditation is to gather those virtues and make them our own.

The division of the twenty mysteries into joyful, luminous, sorrowful, and glorious reflects a grand universal truth about life. All of us will experience moments of joy, light, sorrow, and glory. This is a spiritual law akin to the laws of nature. We can no more escape it than we can the law of gravity. The balance of joy, light, sorrow, and glory is part of the balance of the cosmos. Like the laws of nature, the spiritual laws of the rosary go about their business whether or not we understand, dislike, or agree with them.

The purpose of meditating on the mysteries is to rest in the loving presence of God. We embrace the mysteries and imitate the example of Christ and the Blessed Mother in order to bring them into our daily lives more and more. Their example equips us for the experiences that life will bring. Natural law states that the basic elements of the universe are water, earth, air, and fire. The careful combination of these things makes life possible. Rosary meditation teaches us that the basic elements of the spiritual life are joy, light, sorrow, and glory. The careful combination of these four makes eternal life possible.

We Joyfully Adore: The Joyful Mysteries

*People struggling to know what God is doing in them
remember that woman who knew God's action in
its most profound manner. So, with a sense of
extraordinary release, discovery, companionship,
we find ourselves saying: Hail Mary, full of grace,
the Lord is with thee—and with me, in my way, and
so, blessed are we among women. Pray for me now,
because now I'm beginning to know what you know.
Help me to know it more fully, to bring it to birth.*

—Rosemary Haughton
From *Feminine Spirituality: Reflections on the
Mysteries of the Rosary*

When I think of joyfulness I immediately think of one of my
favorite melodies, Beethoven's "Ode to Joy"—the conclusion to
his great Ninth Symphony. American composer and writer
Henry Van Dyke used Beethoven's melody for his well-known
hymn "Joyful, Joyful, We Adore Thee." Following are some of
the hymn's lyrics:

Joyful, joyful, we adore thee
God of glory, Lord of love;
hearts unfold like flowers before thee,
opening to the sun above.
Melt the clouds of sin and sadness,
drive the dark of doubt away;
giver of immortal gladness;
fill us with the light of day!

The images within these lyrics have always struck me. Van Dyke captured with perfect clarity the kind of joy we experience when we bask in the light of the Lord, the source of light and life on which we all depend. As a kid, after having sung that song at Mass, I would walk out of church just swimming in those lyrics, feeling full of light. In my imagination, I was an unfolding little flower turning my face toward heaven, allowing God to shower his warm light down on me until it poured out of my eyes and mouth and shot out through my fingertips. I was in awe of this image of light driving away the dark of doubt. It was a powerful image.

The song became my own Magnificat. The energy and life that flowed through me were inspired by more than just youthful pleasure. I have never forgotten the power and joy I felt when I sang those words along with a church full of people. I still experience those emotions every time I sing that song for a wedding or at Mass.

It is no small coincidence that I am writing these words while sitting in the house of a friend who is a descendant of Henry Van Dyke—the man who penned those powerful lyrics. My friend is also a songwriter and artist whose personal lineage is rich with artists, writers, poets, and philosophers. It is also no small coincidence that the descendant of the person who wrote a hymn that has such meaning for me has turned out to be my friend. God goes to great lengths to bring joy to our lives.

My friend and I became acquainted through a prayer group. For more than a year, we prayed about the most intimate details of each other's lives, and so it's no surprise to me that I feel a spiritual connection with her while wandering through the halls of her home, eating in her kitchen, and sleeping in her bed. When you stay in someone's home, you gather a sense of what kinds of spiritual things go on there. She has left behind little whispers of her spirit—her creativity, the longings of her heart, her gentleness, her penchant for still and quiet nooks and crannies fit for long afternoons of reading and naps. Hers is a home that has been prayed in often, and a peacefulness lingers here even when she is away.

As I write about the joyful mysteries in this place of joy, I am reminded of another "coincidence" that I do not believe was a work of chance.

I went to graduate school in Alaska. I loved the state, but at times I felt as lonely and cut off from the rest of the world as a NASA lander on the surface of Mars. At such times, I turned to

music for solace. I was comforted countless times by one specific album and one song in particular. "This heart of mine is
yours," it said. I loved the beautiful, weighty lyrics that read like
a prayer and the lush background vocals that accompanied
them.

Some years later I was in Nashville, occasionally singing
background vocals for various artists. Often I sang with a young
man whose talent I greatly admired. His name was Chance, and
he was a freckled redhead from Atlanta, a real southern boy,
funny and charming. We became quite close pals, often singing
together at various gigs around town because our voices
blended nicely and we worked well together. One night out on
a gig, we began sharing about our past experiences and our favorite tunes, the ones that meant the most to us, and I mentioned the song that had meant so much to me in Alaska. I
added that it was especially meaningful because I'd found the
background vocals so soothing and beautiful.

Chance stopped dead in his tracks, eyes wide, and said, "I
sang those background vocals." We looked at each other for a
moment, and then he added, "That's me you were listening to!"

A year later I recorded the song myself. I had Chance sing
the background vocals, once again.

One could argue that these things were coincidences, that I
ended up working with Chance and becoming friends with
Henry Van Dyke's descendant because we are drawn to people
with whom we share something. But I think it's more than that.
I think these are examples of the ways that God delivers joy—in

new life, in new relationships, in pairings that seem unlikely, in circumstances that seem impossible. Part of the delight comes from recognizing the planning as well as the Planner. Like someone at a surprise party thrown in his or her honor, we're tempted to say, "For me?" The resounding response from heaven is always "Yes, my child! Just for you!"

Mary understood that. She opened herself to God's will. The Holy Spirit came upon her to find a holy and wholly prepared vessel for Christ. And she welcomed God completely, without reservation. Mary possessed a love so pure and so full of perfect longing for God that Christ felt immediately at home. The way he and Mary affected each other, sharing their lives and their blood, was the most holy and intimate kind of exchange. She prayed the Magnificat exuberantly—"He has filled the hungry with good things." I like to think that she felt as I felt after singing "Joyful, Joyful, We Adore Thee"—delighted, with light overflowing from her eyes, fingertips, toes.

To meditate on the joyful mysteries is to be innocently delighted and surprised. It is to find promise in the most unlikely places, to celebrate an unmatchable intimate union. It is to understand that God will work out his promises, but only if we will continually say yes to his loving company and direction, only if we will continually search out his presence in every circumstance. He is just waiting to surprise us with the promises he keeps.

Come into these joyful mysteries and be prepared to make a joyful noise.

First Joyful Mystery: The Annunciation

In the sixth month the angel Gabriel was sent by God to a town in Galilee called Nazareth, to a virgin engaged to a man whose name was Joseph, of the house of David. The virgin's name was Mary. And he came to her and said, "Greetings, favored one! The Lord is with you." But she was much perplexed by his words and pondered what sort of greeting this might be. The angel said to her, "Do not be afraid, Mary, for you have found favor with God. And now, you will conceive in your womb and bear a son, and you will name him Jesus. He will be great, and will be called the Son of the Most High, and the Lord God will give to him the throne of his ancestor David. He will reign over the house of Jacob forever, and of his kingdom there will be no end." Mary said to the angel, "How can this be, since I am a virgin?" The angel said to her, "The Holy Spirit will come upon you, and the power of the Most High will overshadow you; therefore the child to be born will be holy; he will be called Son of God. And now, your relative Elizabeth in her old age has also conceived a son; and this is the sixth month for her who was said to be barren. For nothing will be impossible with God." Then Mary said, "Here am I, the servant of the Lord; let it be with me according to your word." Then the angel departed from her. (Luke 1:26–38)

Scripture tells us nothing about the physical setting of the Annunciation. Rather, it concentrates on emotion: first confusion and fear, then surrender and joy.

It was a moment long awaited and hoped for—the entrance of the Word made flesh, the Redeemer, into human history, made possible by that gentle yes. Lord, be it done unto me according to your word. What tremendous faith must have dwelt within her to say yes without knowing the final outcome, without assurance for her worldly provision in such an unusual circumstance. Still, Mary never questioned the word except to ask how it might be possible.

> *Father, each day you invite me to align my will with yours. Each day I have the opportunity to bring Christ more into the world, or not. Yet often I immediately question your more challenging entreaties. Teach me your voice. Help me to become aware of the invitations you bring to me each day so that I too might have courage and say yes. Help me to give birth to all that you have planned for me. Come and make your home in me too.*
>
> *I pray for the virtue of faith.*

The Second Joyful Mystery: The Visitation

In those days Mary set out and went with haste to a Judean town in the hill country, where she entered the house of Zechariah and greeted Elizabeth. When Elizabeth heard Mary's greeting, the child leaped in her womb. And Elizabeth was filled with the Holy Spirit and exclaimed with a loud cry, "Blessed are you among women, and blessed is the fruit of your womb. And why has this happened to me, that the mother of my Lord comes to me? For as soon as I heard the sound of your greeting, the child in my womb leaped for joy. And blessed is she who believed that there would be a fulfillment of what was spoken to her by the Lord."

And Mary said, "My soul magnifies the Lord, and my spirit rejoices in God my Savior, for he has looked with favor on the lowliness of his servant. Surely, from now on all generations will call me blessed; for the Mighty One has done great things for me, and holy is his name. His mercy is for those who fear him from generation to generation. He has shown strength with his arm; he has scattered the proud in the thoughts of their hearts. He has brought down the powerful from their thrones, and lifted up the lowly; he has filled the hungry with good things, and sent the rich away empty. He has helped his servant Israel, in remembrance of his mercy, according to the promise he made to our ancestors, to Abraham and to his descendants forever."

And Mary remained with her about three months and then returned to her home. (Luke 1:39–56)

Mary's Magnificat is a unique moment of eloquence. To share the intimate revelation she has just received, she first runs to her cousin Elizabeth—another woman whose pregnancy should not have been possible. "My spirit rejoices!" she says to her cousin, and in that, "Won't you rejoice with me too?" That has been the cry of Mary's heart. "See what good things the Lord has done for me. See how he has kept his promises. See what might do for you, how he might keep his promises for and within you too. Let's rejoice together!"

You are a God who keeps your promises. You will complete your virtues in me.

Father, I long to be the kind of friend to whom others rush to share their most intimate and profound news. May I be blessed with the joy of experiencing such rich friendships. Let the foundation of my friendships always be the sharing of the joy you bring to us, the fulfillment of your promise. Open my eyes to the people around me so that I see them for the precious gifts that they really are. Remind me that charity is first an action.

I pray for the virtue of charity, that deep filial love.

The Third Joyful Mystery: The Birth of Jesus

In those days a decree went out from Emperor Augustus that all the world should be registered. This was the first registration and was taken while Quirinius was governor of Syria. All went to their own towns to be registered. Joseph also went from the town of Nazareth in Galilee to Judea, to the city of David called Bethlehem, because he was descended from the house and family of David. He went to be registered with Mary, to whom he was engaged and who was expecting a child. While they were there, the time came for her to deliver her child. And she gave birth to her firstborn son and wrapped him in bands of cloth, and laid him in a manger, because there was no place for them in the inn.

In that region there were shepherds living in the fields, keeping watch over their flock by night. Then an angel of the Lord stood before them, and the glory of the Lord shone around them, and they were terrified. But the angel said to them, "Do not be afraid; for see—I am bringing you good news of great joy for all the people: to you is born this day in the city of David a Savior, who is the Messiah, the Lord. This will be a sign for you: you will find a child wrapped in bands of cloth and lying in a manger." And suddenly there was with the angel a multitude of the heavenly host, praising God and saying, "Glory to God in the highest heaven, and on earth peace among those whom he favors!"

When the angels had left them and gone into heaven, the shepherds said to one another, "Let us go now to Bethlehem and see this thing that has taken place, which the Lord has made known to us." So they went with haste and found Mary and Joseph, and the child lying in the manger. When they saw this, they made known what had been told them about this child; and all who heard it were amazed at what the shepherds told them. But Mary treasured all these words and pondered them in her heart. (Luke 2:1–19)

Until this point, Mary has had the child entirely to herself. Now, in front of an audience largely made up of animals, she brings him forth into the world, just as God promised. How astonishing it must have been to finally meet her infant, her Savior, face-to-face.

> *Lord, I am always looking for the obvious answer. I think I know what a messiah should look like, with accommodations*

and accoutrements that suit a king. Your choices are so surprising—first this simple Jewish girl and now this humble stable. I am learning to keep my eyes open to expect the unexpected and to see that the simple, humble thing is often more valuable than it may appear on the outside, that it is often your greatest work of art.

You, O Lord, are often a God of quiet mystery, of humble intrigue. Please welcome me in my childlike faith into your wondrous, magnificent plan of salvation, into the birth of your will. Deafen my screaming pride. Broaden my vision to embrace the unexpected. Thank you for the gift of life, the miracle of creativity.

I pray for the virtue of humility and to greatly desire it.

A Joyful Solution

Joe is a successful triathlete and an attorney who practices law in a very demanding industry in a major Midwestern city. Growing up Catholic, he had some experience of the rosary in school and at home, but he didn't really begin to practice the meditation in earnest until his early thirties. He did so because he sought relief from the intense pressures of balancing work and home life.

When he first started praying the rosary, he would often ask for specific answers to his prayers, almost like a reward.

"I would think, 'Okay, I've made my payment,'" says Joe, "'now I should get it,' whatever 'it' was. But now I pray more for the grace to understand what God wants me to do and for the grace and courage to do it."

Like many rosary devotees, his attitude about prayer and meditation shifted as he continued to practice the meditation.

"My perception of what God wants me to do tunes in as I pray," he says. "As I go through the rosary thinking about the life of Jesus, I'm trying to be open to perceptions and feelings. Inevitably, new ways of resolving some issues that I'm facing come into my mind."

Recently, he experienced just this—a simple answer to a rather perplexing situation. The unmarried nanny of his two young girls discovered that she was pregnant. Although the young woman had decided to marry the father of her child at a later date, the pregnancy caused a great deal of trauma for her and her family. The would-be grandparents were already thinking of the child in a very negative light. The inevitable birth of the child, something that should be a joyous occasion, was causing division and sadness. Joe also worried about the effect of this crisis on his two young girls.

While praying the rosary one day, Joe had an idea. Why shouldn't his nanny and her boyfriend get married right now? A number of practical difficulties seemed to stand in the way of that, not least of which was his reticence to help. Initially it was tempting for Joe to just walk away from the situation. He was concerned for his own children, and the situation created a strained environment in his house. But after praying, Joe thought that maybe he and his wife could help remove some of the obstacles. "[I thought] that that baby really deserved a life, to have things start off well."

Joe and his wife offered their house for the ceremony and the reception and money to cover the wedding expenses. Their nanny was entirely receptive. The couple had a joyous wedding.

Not surprisingly, Joe's favorite mystery is the third joyful mystery, the Nativity.

"I think the birth of Christ is my favorite because it's so innocent," says Joe. "Innocence is a virtue, to be more child-like, and I like that simplicity. Here's this great thing out of utter simplicity. I like that notion."

The Fourth Joyful Mystery: The Presentation

When the time came for their purification according to the law of Moses, they brought him up to Jerusalem to present him to the Lord (as it is written in the law of the Lord, "Every firstborn male shall be designated as holy to the Lord"), and they offered a sacrifice according to what is stated in the law of the Lord, "a pair of turtledoves or two young pigeons."

Now there was a man in Jerusalem whose name was Simeon; this man was righteous and devout, looking forward to the consolation of Israel, and the Holy Spirit rested on him. It had been revealed to him by the Holy Spirit that he would not see death before he had seen the Lord's Messiah. Guided by the Spirit, Simeon came into the temple; and when the parents brought in the child Jesus, to do for him what was customary under the law, Simeon took him in his arms and praised God, saying, "Master, now you are dismissing your servant in peace, according to your word; for my eyes have seen your salvation, which you have prepared in the presence of all peoples, a light for revelation to the Gentiles and for glory to your people Israel."

And the child's father and mother were amazed at what was being said about him. Then Simeon blessed them and said to his mother Mary, "This child is destined for the falling and the rising of many in Israel, and to be a sign that will be opposed so that the inner thoughts of many will be revealed—and a sword will pierce your own soul too."

There was also a prophet, Anna the daughter of Phanuel, of the tribe of Asher. She was of a great age, having lived with her husband seven years after her marriage, then as a widow to the age of eighty-four. She never left the temple but worshiped there with fasting and prayer night and day. At that moment she came, and began to praise God and to speak about the child to all who were looking for the redemption of Jerusalem.

When they had finished everything required by the law of the Lord, they returned to Galilee, to their own town of Nazareth. (Luke 2:22–39)

We've just come from the birth, where we've been steeped in the infinite possibility of new life. The presentation offers us the first foreshadowing, the first bittersweet taste of the sorrow that is to come. A sword will pierce the heart of the Blessed Mother and anyone who accepts Christ.

The presentation is an act of obedience, but it is also a part of the process of recognition and identification. Once again, when the holy family says yes to the law, they make possible the ultimate yes that God says to us: "Yes, I recognize you; yes, you are my child and may enter into my dwelling place for all eternity." But first we must present ourselves; we must allow God to establish rightful ownership of his creation.

Lord, to whom do I say I belong? Who do I say owns me, heart and soul? I pray for the virtue of obedience, yes. But I also pray that I might present myself to you daily as your property to do with as you will. I pray that daily I might bring to you all that I am—my talents, the longings of my heart, my goals—and present myself to you for you to design. In your mercy, you prepared the hearts of the holy family to accept that there would be pain ahead. Remind me that your will for me will involve pain and sacrifice, but that I may rest assured that, if I continue to present myself to you, you will be there at the end of my life to say, "Yes, I know you; you are mine."

Lord, I am your creation, your property, designed to serve you. Give me the grace to present myself to you daily to do your will.

The Fifth Joyful Mystery: Finding the Child Jesus in the Temple

The child grew and became strong, filled with wisdom; and the favor of God was upon him.

Now every year his parents went to Jerusalem for the festival of the Passover. And when he was twelve years old, they went up as usual for the festival. When the festival was ended and they started to return, the boy Jesus stayed behind in Jerusalem, but his parents did not know it. Assuming that he was in the group of travelers, they went a day's journey. Then they started to look for him among their relatives and friends. When they did not find him, they returned to Jerusalem to search for him. After three days they found him in the temple, sitting among the teachers, listening to them and asking them questions. And all who heard him were amazed at his understanding and his answers. When his parents saw him they were astonished; and his mother said to him, "Child, why have you treated us like this? Look, your father and I have been searching for you in great anxiety." He said to them, "Why were you searching for me? Did you not know that I must be in my Father's house?" But they did not understand what he said to them. Then he went down with them and came to Nazareth, and was obedient to them. His mother treasured all these things in her heart.

And Jesus increased in wisdom and in years, and in divine and human favor. (Luke 2:40–52)

The inevitable separation has begun: Jesus is nearly a teenager, beginning to "leave home." But where does he go?

Directly to his Father's house. He lived and grew in the house of Mary's womb, and when it was time she gave birth to him. Then he lived and grew in the house of the holy family, and when it was time he left there too. The joy of this mystery is what we find in our Father's house: the shelter of wisdom.

Lord, where am I looking for wisdom? Where may I find the answers to my questions? Help me to remember that I will only find wisdom in the Word made flesh and in your house, your temple. Let me run to both.

Let me ever desire your presence. Mary and Joseph found their most precious possession in the temple. I will too.

Today, I want to bring all my precious possessions—my belongings, my relationships, my vocation, my loved ones— and present them to you. Keep them all safe in your house, the house of wisdom, peace, and salvation.

I pray for the gift of wisdom.

An Ordinary Saint

Some holy people, like the renowned Padre Pio, seemed to have no trouble practicing rosary devotion. But many do. One such person was the young, unassuming French Carmelite nun St. Thérèse of Lisieux, also called the Little Flower or St. Thérèse of the Child Jesus. Although she was deeply devoted to the Blessed Mother, St. Thérèse sometimes spoke of how difficult the practice of rosary devotion was for her and how strongly she believed that she failed to pray it well.

St. Thérèse's life was short and spent mostly in seclusion. She entered the Carmelite order at age fifteen and spent nine years in convent life before dying at the age of twenty-four. She had contracted tuberculosis and had spent the last months of her life in agony, coughing up blood and suffering great pain, often near suffocation.

Though her life seemed quiet from the outside, she had a rich interior life. Before she died, St. Thérèse wrote her autobiography, *Story of a Soul,* which chronicles her spiritual path with enormous passion. She modeled her intercession after that of the Blessed Mother. Her autobiography, her letters, and her last conversations, which were recorded by the sisters who sat with her, all reveal a person in search of Jesus, a person burning with an ardent desire for holiness and with a truly childlike faith, or what she called "the little way of spiritual childhood."

"I do like children who do not know how to read," she wrote in her autobiography. "I say very simply to God what I wish to say without composing beautiful sentences." Although the rosary prayers are very simple to say, St. Thérèse recognized their depth. She wrote: "I feel I have said it so poorly! I force myself in vain to meditate on the mysteries of the rosary; I don't succeed in fixing my mind on them."

St. Thérèse eventually found ways to embrace the rosary. She slowed down and concentrated on one prayer at a time.

"I very slowly recite an 'Our Father' and then the angelic salutation; then these prayers give me great delight; they nourish my soul much more than if I had recited them precipitately a hundred times."

The sisters of her Carmelite order prayed vigorous and nearly continuous rosary novenas to Our Lady of Victory during Thérèse's final illness. If the "victory" of one's death is measured by how peacefully one is able to accept it, St. Thérèse died a very victorious death. She was completely devoted to the Blessed Mother and in her final months displayed extraordinary courage. In one of the conversations that was recorded from her bedside by another sister, she said, "It's not 'death' that will come in search of me, it's God. Death isn't some phantom, some horrible specter, as it is represented in pictures. It is said in the *Catechism* that 'death is the separation of the soul from the body' and that is all it is." While her suffering was extreme to the very end, her final words, which she uttered while looking at a crucifix, are recorded as "My God! I love you!"

St. Thérèse was canonized in 1925, declared Patroness of the Missions in 1927, and declared a doctor of the church in 1997. She is only the second woman to have received the title of doctor of the church.

Holding the Lamp:
The Luminous Mysteries

The thing about light is that it really isn't yours; it's
what you gather and shine back. And it gets more
power from reflectiveness; if you sit still and take it in,
it fills your cup, and then you can give it off yourself.
—Anne Lamott, *Traveling Mercies*

When I really need to find my way, there are few places more
helpful to me than the ocean. The sound and smell of the surf,
the tides that swell and encroach to swallow up and then release the rocky shore beneath it, a perpetual game of tag between water and murky earth, each taking turn being "it". These
things bring me stillness and often, "the still small voice."

I am especially fond of the rocky volcanic-gray beaches
of Maine. And at my favorite ocean perch, there sits on an
island just offshore, a short, fat, sturdy-looking little white lighthouse. I have spent many hours staring out across those steely
Atlantic waves, pondering that lonely little tower, retired now
from truly active duty with advances in sonar and other tools

for navigation. But, in its day, what a mighty, intriguing job it had—perpetually casting out its light to those in darkness.

Situated where water meets dry land, the lighthouse announces transition, a change in the territory ahead, as if to say, "Prepare, be alert, the coast is coming!" The lighthouse helps us to navigate transition at the most significant, sometimes most tumultuous, point in our journey. Whether on the coast of ocean, lake, or river, it is a welcome harbinger that home is near and a powerful instrument providing direction and guidance through various hazards of weather and topography. The lonely lighthouse, quiet and constant and often standing alone, comes to mind as I meditate upon the luminous mysteries, the public ministry of Christ.

Navigating this life has its hazards too. Clouded, foggy thinking can take us off course. Treacherous embedded rocks of resentment and bitterness might reach up within us to tear us apart. Windless seas and seasons where we seem to go nowhere might convince us that futility reigns and nothing will ever change. Tides of grief, disappointment, and fear may wash over us and weigh us down so deeply that we lose hope of ever rising up out of the water again. We need our own lighthouses, luminaries to show us the way, to help us move forward in our spiritual life, to guide us through the transition, transformation, and change that mark the life of anyone who chooses to follow Christ.

In the luminous mysteries, Christ announces himself as "the light of the world," our ultimate source of direction, burning with a perpetual love for God's children. In fact, the *Catechism* teaches us that in baptism, we are named "daughters and sons of light." Christ makes himself manifest to us in all of the sacraments, and baptism, reconciliation, and Holy Communion are important sacraments contained within the meditations of the luminous mysteries.

But Christ also makes himself manifest to us by those who "put on Christ," those who carry his light and his message to us: *You are loved.* In so doing, they guide us to the safe and sacred shores of acceptance and love and holy purpose.

I think first of my parents who carry the message by lending me their faith and confidence when mine runs low. Their lives, full of constant sacrifice and selflessness, have been shining examples to me, blessing my life with abundance beyond measure. I think of myriad friends who have loved me through moments when I was intolerably negative, self-centered, and oh-so-prickly to the touch. There were teachers and coaches who helped me to believe I was worth something in the attention they paid, and professors who helped me to refine my gifts so I could give them to the world. There have been mentors, further down the spiritual path, calling out, "Follow me, come this way!"

Because of these luminaries, I can shine in the dark for others too. As my radiant friend and one of my greatest luminaries, Cristia, says: "We take turns holding the lamp for each other." She has held it up for me, bright and brilliant and inviting, more times than I can count.

In fact, Cristia stands a bit like a lighthouse, only not like a short, scrappy utilitarian one with moss or barnacles growing on its chubby trunks. Cristia is of the regal, elegant, lovely variety that claims its appointment on rocky ocean peaks with deep, feminine authority and grace. Her warm light, a natural extension of her, filled with purpose and true things, reaching far out into foggy, chilly places. She is tall and lean and possesses a gentle constancy in her comportment. Crowned with a lovely wave of thick gray hair, into which her hairdresser occasionally sprinkles "goldy-bits," I have thought on more than one occasion that Cristia actually does glow.

She also possesses the greatest clarity of thought of anyone I have ever known. She has helped to lead me through my own spiritual growing pains with startling acuity, parting the clouds of my troubled heart on the most delicate and difficult issues of my life. Our theologies may part their ways from time to time, but they always seem to travel out and circle back again, and we find ourselves bumping into each other often on these sacred, mystical planes where souls go looking for God's will and wisdom, comfort and company. Two women most earnestly seeking our heavenly marching orders, "pawns in training," we say.

Cristia is a visionary. Her genius is to see in others talents and abilities they may not see themselves. This is a luminous gift. She further helps to draw these talents and abilities out of people so they may use them to help others. I know because she has done this for me. She tells me that through my gifts she has seen me be Christ to others, "like an angel" she says, but it almost makes me laugh. I feel like a dimly lit little matchstick next to the glorious Olympic torch I see her to be, and to hear her say that makes me think, but you're the one named *Cristia!*

But torch or matchstick, which is brighter is not the point. The point is that a dark room isn't as dark when we're *both* burning in it.

All of the luminous mysteries build to the same gentle, poignant pinnacle in the institution of the Eucharist.

Holy Communion is the deepest mystery of our faith and probably the most misunderstood, even by practicing Catholics. The transubstantiation, or the changing of the bread and wine into the Body and Blood, can be a confusing, even frightening concept, and I'd earnestly recommend that you discuss any questions you might have with a well-studied, prayerful Catholic. In short, the church teaches us that "the Eucharist nourishes the disciple with Christ's Body and Blood for his transformation in Christ." We believe that the Christian life is marked by movement of the soul toward Christ, that Jesus is truly present to us in the Eucharist, and that the sacrifice of the Mass is the same sacrifice he made on Calvary—not an additional one, but the same one.

At the Last Supper, when the quiet innocence and sacred intimacy of the joyful mysteries have matured, Jesus changes the very nature of bread and wine to Body and Blood. And then, astoundingly, he turns to the guests at the table, offers them this miraculous sacrifice, and issues a perpetual invitation: "Do this in remembrance of me." And in so doing, he passes the lamp on to you and to me. He beckons, "Do not forget, choose to remember what I have named you in baptism: beloved sons and daughters of light. Choose to remember my path. Come back to it in Holy Communion. You are all invited."

Christ offers himself to us, a luminous gift. This Jesus. He is not for safekeeping, locked away in a vault with a combination you keep forgetting, not a forgotten cheap trinket stored on the top shelf of a remote and dusty closet in the house. This gift is not like your good shoes that you wear only to church on Sunday or like a Christmas candle you burn only once a year. Accepting this gift will change us from the inside out, will make our whole lives "a new creature" at their very foundations. Our whole lives, our everyday, do-the-laundry, go-to-school, pay-bills, walk-the-dog, go-to-work kind of lives can become a living sacrifice, sacramental and sacred, burning and effervescent, luminous. We receive the body of Christ in order to become the Mystical Body of Christ to the world.

The luminous mysteries point to the dual nature of Christian life: giving and receiving, it is a Holy Communion. They call us out of the hidden life of preparation to be creatures of light in a dark world. As it is with my friend Cristia, it can be a great joy to witness others as they flourish after our own experience and wisdom. But be forewarned, being a luminary among creatures trapped in darkness isn't always easy and may not make you wildly popular. It is an act of outright heroism to walk into a dark room when you feel like a dimly lit little match. But sacramental lives are demanding, and luminaries who announce the need for change are often met with fierce criticism and resistance. Don't be too surprised if, along the way, you feel a little lonely, a seeming lighthouse unto nothing and no one, with nary a ship in sight. The heartiest of our luminary saints often experienced feelings of loneliness, doubt, abandonment, and futility. The irony remains: in order to keep this great treasure, we must give it away. Like Christ at the Last Supper, we must accept the invitation to the table, and then become a living invitation to others to join us in sacramental lives.

No matter where you are in your spiritual journey, make a decision, choose to remember that you are deeply loved and that the light and grace of heaven can reach you even in the darkest, coldest places to guide you safely to God's presence. There you will find acceptance and love, comfort and wisdom and healing, the warm and holy shores of home.

Bring whatever light you have with you when you come. Don't worry if it's dim. There will be other lights there too. And we have luminous work to do.

The First Luminous Mystery: The Baptism of Jesus

Then Jesus came from Galilee to John at the Jordan, to be baptized by him. John would have prevented him, saying, "I need to be baptized by you, and do you come to me?" But Jesus answered him, "Let it be so now; for it is proper for us in this way to fulfill all righteousness." Then he consented. And when Jesus had been baptized, just as he came up from the water, suddenly the heavens were opened to him and he saw the Spirit of God descending like a dove and alighting on him. And a voice from heaven said, "This is my Son, the Beloved, with whom I am well pleased." (Matthew 3:13–17)

It is the first of our most treasured sacraments, and the entrance point of Christ into his public ministry. Prepared, anointed, and claimed by heaven as the beloved and pleasing Son, Christ enters fully into the Father's plan. In complete acceptance and surrender, at the appointed time, having fulfilled all righteousness, Jesus emerges from the water: *Messiah.*

Baptism is an entrance into heaven's plan for us too. *The Catechism of the Catholic Church* teaches us that "the person baptized has been 'enlightened,' he becomes a 'son of light,' indeed, he becomes 'light' himself" (#1216). It teaches that baptism "not only purifies from all sins, but also makes the neophyte 'a new creature,' an adopted son of God, who has become a 'partaker of the divine nature,' (#1265). The baptized "share in the priesthood of Christ, in his prophetic and royal mission" (#1268).

We are new creatures; royal, purified, divine, priestly people walking as new creatures in the light of our baptismal promise. The spirit of heaven is available to come and alight upon us all, to welcome us all as sons and daughters of light, to call us all by name: *Beloved.*

> *Oh, sweet spirit from heaven, you come to alight on me, to wash me in forgiveness, and name me your beloved. With delight and overwhelming gratitude, I accept your gift of*

*grace, to become a new, luminous creature! Today, free me
from anything keeping me from becoming your daughter of
light. Release me at the appointed time to fulfill all your
priestly plans for me.*

*I pray for the gift to remember that you have called me
your beloved, and that you have a plan for me, a priestly
appointment. May I be open to the Holy Spirit.*

The Second Luminous Mystery: The Wedding at Cana

*On the third day there was a wedding in Cana of Galilee, and the
mother of Jesus was there. Jesus and his disciples had also been invited to the wedding. When the wine gave out, the mother of Jesus
said to him, "They have no wine." And Jesus said to her, "Woman,
what concern is that to you and to me? My hour has not yet come."
His mother said to the servants, "Do whatever he tells you." Now,
standing there were six stone water jars for the Jewish rites of purification, each holding twenty or thirty gallons. Jesus said to them, "Fill
the jars with water." And they filled them up to the brim. He said to
them, "Now draw some out, and take it to the chief steward." So they
took it. When the steward tasted the water that had become wine, and
did not know where it came from (though the servants who had drawn
the water knew), the steward called the bridegroom and said to him,
"Everyone serves the good wine first, and then the inferior wine after
the guests have become drunk. But you have kept the good wine until
now." Jesus did this, the first of his signs, in Cana of Galilee, and
revealed his glory; and his disciples believed in him. (John 2:1–11)*

Water becomes wine, a miracle. In this rich passage, John captures the power of God to transform us, to change the very nature of things. The wedding at Cana announces Christ as Messiah and shows us that when we bring our needs to God, he satisfies beyond our comprehension.

It also captures the beauty and necessity of surrendering to God's authority completely. "Do whatever he tells you," says Mary. The resulting life of abundance and blessing that follows that surrender is more generous and of a higher, more authentic quality than what we could ever manage on our own.

> *Jesus, just like Mary at the wedding feast, I bring my needs to you in this meditation. I believe that your way, sweet Jesus, leads to plenty when there is deprivation, to provision where there is need, to sanity and peace where there is chaos and confusion, to refinement and quality where I would have settled for less, to miracles where there is no reason to hope. Let me put aside my own self-will, fear, and doubt, and instead, do your will always, trusting that you will bless in unexpected, abundant ways.*
>
> *I pray for greater trust and for the virtue of surrender.*

The Third Luminous Mystery: Proclaiming the Kingdom

As you go, proclaim the good news, "The kingdom of heaven has come near." Cure the sick, raise the dead, cleanse the lepers, cast out demons. You received without payment; give without payment. (Matthew 10:7–8)

Most of us will never cleanse a leper, but we can speak words of healing and comfort to a suffering world. We may never cast out demons, but we can cast out fear, doubt, unforgiveness, and insecurity from our relationships. We may never raise a dead man to life, but we can choose life every day by remembering God's message of love. We can tell the world in everyday ways: God loves you and desires your company. You were created to share in the abundance of the divine life.

> *The surest way to keep something I have is to give it away. Jesus, help me to live a life of service, and as Mother Teresa says, "do ordinary things with extraordinary love." Help me to carry the message in everyday ways; in even small ways, let me be "light in the world." Let me be your vessel, bringing those in darkness home to safe harbors. Today, open my heart to see the ways that I can proclaim the kingdom, to give without pay, to forgive as I have been forgiven.*
>
> *I pray for a servant's heart, and for opportunity.*

The Fourth Luminous Mystery: The Transfiguration

Now about eight days after these sayings Jesus took with him Peter and John and James, and went up on the mountain to pray. And while he was praying, the appearance of his face changed, and his clothes became dazzling white. Suddenly they saw two men, Moses and Elijah, talking to him. They appeared in glory and were speaking of his departure, which he was about to accomplish at Jerusalem. Now Peter and his companions were weighed down with sleep; but

since they had stayed awake, they saw his glory and the two men
who stood with him. Just as they were leaving him, Peter said to
Jesus, "Master, it is good for us to be here; let us make three dwellings,
one for you, one for Moses, and one for Elijah"—not knowing what
he said. While he was saying this, a cloud came and overshadowed
them; and they were terrified as they entered the cloud. Then from
the cloud came a voice that said, "This is my Son, my Chosen; listen
to him!" When the voice had spoken, Jesus was found alone. And they
kept silent and in those days told no one any of the things they had
seen. (Luke 9: 28–36)

Jesus went up the mountain to pray. He removed himself
from the demands of his public and daily life in order to seek
out the presence of God in a specific, concentrated way. And
that presence transfigured him. That presence will transform us.

This is what makes prayer and the sacraments so powerful.
In the presence of God, we are transformed. God can change
us, can strip away the things of this world that darken our
hearts, and instead make us shining and glorious. When we
take the time to pray, when we climb the mountain, seek him
out, make space to recognize God's presence and listen to him,
the results are dazzling.

> *Jesus, I come to you in this very meditation, my simple way*
> *of "climbing the mountain" into your presence. I ask you to*
> *send the Holy Spirit down upon me to transform me into*
> *your holy, chosen creature. I am here, listening for your*
> *voice, earnestly inviting your friendship. Make me your*
> *pawn; show me my purpose.*

I pray for the determination to wait for you in prayer, to listen, and for the willingness to change.

The Fifth Luminous Mystery: Institution of the Eucharist

When the hour came, he took his place at the table, and the apostles with him. He said to them, "I have eagerly desired to eat this Passover with you before I suffer; for I tell you, I will not eat it until it is fulfilled in the kingdom of God." Then he took a cup, and after giving thanks he said, "Take this and divide it among yourselves; for I tell you that from now on I will not drink of the fruit of the vine until the kingdom of God comes." Then he took a loaf of bread, and when he had given thanks, he broke it and gave it to them, saying, "This is my body, which is given for you. Do this in remembrance of me." And he did the same with the cup after supper, saying, "This cup that is poured out for you is the new covenant in my blood." (Luke 22:14–20)

Christ was eager to share the Passover meal with his disciples. He was eager to invite them to take and eat, and to remember. Every time we participate in the Mass, every time we choose to remember, we are taken up into the very mystery and miracle of God to reconcile our nature with his. We accept the gift eagerly offered, and we become new creatures, priestly people, people who hold up the lamp for one another.

The hour has come. You are being invited. Will you take your place at the table? Will you come in remembrance? There is a space reserved for the one and only you.

Jesus, I accept your invitation. I believe you are truly pres-
ent to me and that your presence will heal me where I am
sick, strengthen me where I am weak, purify me where I
need forgiveness, guide me where I am lost, and comfort me
when I am hurting. I accept your invitation to remember
your sacrifice and to join you in your royal mission as your
child of light to those lost in dark and cold places.

I pray for an adoring, luminous heart.

Living Visitation

She was a geography teacher, a tireless servant to the smallest,
the weakest, the poor; an uncompromising advocate of the
unborn, the unwanted, the unloved. Pope John Paul II called
her "a feminine genius;" Professor Carol Zeleski said she was a
"twentieth-century commander of a worldwide apostolate and
army of charity." The world called her "mother." Diminutive
in stature, a simple, humble immigrant, and Nobel Peace
Prize winner, Mother Teresa was perhaps the most beloved,
paradoxical, and influential luminary of our time.

Born in 1910 in what was then Turkey, Agnes Gonxha
Bojaxhiu was raised by Albanian Roman Catholic parents.
Her father was murdered when she was just seven years old.
At eighteen, she joined the Sisters of Loretto in Ireland, a
teaching order, and was soon sent to India. After nearly
twenty years teaching, Mother Teresa entered a period of profound "divine union" that has tied her to the lives and traditions of the mystics. For nearly two years, she experienced

interior locutions and visions of Jesus. In these extraordinary divine exchanges, Mother Teresa received concrete instructions to establish an order of Indian nuns, who would go into the slums carrying Christ's "fire of love amongst the poor, the sick, the dying, and the little children."

The Missionaries of Charity opened their first home in India in 1952 on the Feast of the Immaculate Heart of Mary. Over the next five decades, the Missionaries would open homes for sisters, brothers, lay ministers, and contemplatives throughout the world. Devoted to loving the "unlovable," under the leadership of Mother Teresa's example, these men and women, along with masses of volunteers, would tend to countless prostitutes, lepers, drug addicts, battered women, AIDS patients, unwed mothers, the poor, the orphaned, and the dying. Like Christ, Mother Teresa's public ministry was a powerful catalyst for change.

She often spoke of the necessity of prayer to grace her for a life of service. In fact, the Missionaries of Charity begin each day with prayer and the Mass and end each day with an hour of eucharistic adoration. She also emphasized sincerity and simplicity in prayer.

"If you are searching for God and do not know where to begin," she said, "learn to pray and take the trouble to pray every day. . . . Just speak. Tell him everything, talk to him. He is our father, he is father to us all whatever religion we are. . . . If we pray, we will get all the answers we need."

She was devoted to the Blessed Mother, and the rosary was an integral part of her daily prayer life. Those who spent time close to her have remarked that she never took a step without her rosary beads and that she prayed the rosary quietly and without ceasing, on planes, in meetings, walking the slums of Calcutta. In one moment of intense prayer, Jesus appeared to Mother Teresa, saying, "My little one, come, come, carry me into the holes of the poor. Come, be my light," and in another he specifically instructed her to "teach them to say the Rosary, the family Rosary, and all will be well."

Her favorite mystery was, not surprisingly, the Visitation, where the virtues of charity and service were exemplified in Mary's journey to tend her cousin Elizabeth, an expectant mother.

"The most beautiful thing about Our Lady," said Mother Teresa, "was that when Jesus came into her life, immediately, in haste, she went to St. Elizabeth's place to give Jesus to her and to her Son. . . . How much we can learn from Our Lady! She was so humble because she was all for God. She was full of grace."

Like Jesus, Mother Teresa was not without her opponents. Her highly publicized life came with challenges for her uncompromising messages about "giving until it hurts," her unflinching pro-life stance, and her apparent disinterest in extending the life of the dying, focusing instead on making their final hours ones filled with loving human contact. Characteristic of Mother Teresa's pragmatic approach to living a life of service, she said, "Do not worry about why problems exist in the world—just respond to people's needs."

Nor was Mother Teresa without her own "agony in the garden," moments of excruciating interior pain including profound feelings of abandonment, loneliness, and rejection by God. As revealed by her letters to her spiritual directors following the two-year period of extraordinary divine union and not long after she began the work that she'd been called to in those interior locutions, God's presence was withdrawn from her. This desolation would shadow her for the rest of her life. However, her extraordinary tenacity to love and serve the poor in the face of such desolation only adds to her remarkable mystical appeal and selfless example.

Zaleski writes, "It means that the missionary foundress who called herself 'God's pencil' was not the God-intoxicated saint many of us had assumed her to be. We may prefer to think that she spent her days in a state of ecstatic mystical union with God, because that would get us ordinary worldlings off the hook."

On the contrary, Mother Teresa, a true light to those in darkness, found herself steeped in shadow. Yet she remained determined, her entire being fixed on Jesus, to radiate the love and light of Christ to anyone who needed it, not just the destitute and, as author Bharati Mukherjee so aptly described them, "the pestilential."

Mother Teresa often spoke of the loneliness of the Western world, in which despite having much, people were lonelier than the poor of Calcutta.

"The greatest disease in the West today is not TB or leprosy," she said, "it is being unwanted, unloved, and uncared for. We can cure physical diseases with medicine, but the only cure for loneliness, despair, and hopelessness is love. There are many in the world who are dying for a piece of bread but there are many more dying for a little love. The poverty in the West is a different kind of poverty—it is not only a poverty of loneliness but also of spirituality. There's a hunger for love, as there is a hunger for God."

Mother Teresa died September 5, 1997, and was beatified by Pope John Paul II on October 19, 2003, at the close of the Year of the Rosary.

Sorrow in the Mix: The Sorrowful Mysteries

If the world hates you, be aware that it hated me before it hated you. (John 15:18)

The joyful mysteries are a celebration of the deepest kind of intimacy. In the luminous mysteries, that intimacy is broadened. The sorrowful mysteries, however, seem to rip apart all that has been sewn together. They are sometimes presented as an exercise in stoicism—just bear up under whatever horrific hardship life brings you. But this is not what the sorrowful mysteries have taught me. Instead, they probe the eternal depth and value of grief, suffering, and, when necessary, silent submission.

The sorrowful mysteries also tend to lead to subtle and uncomfortable confrontations with one's own defects. When I think of this, a music review I received several years ago always comes to mind.

I was giving a concert to promote the release of my first CD. Both the concert and the CD were reviewed by a music critic who had virtually nothing positive to say about either. This man had reviewed my work several times before, always negatively.

His primary complaint—and also the headline of his review—was "Kelly lacks restraint." He said that I was talented but that I had a tendency to oversing, to overdo. He said that rather than just letting the song be, I tried too hard to make it something. A decade into my craft, I was pained to read this, but I had to admit that the criticism was accurate. Furthermore, I knew that what the reviewer said of my singing was true of many areas of my life—I always tried to *make* things happen.

I tried to practice the principle about criticism that I taught my own students—look for critics who want to see you succeed, not fail. Look for critics who wish to see the art form thrive. If they truly love the art form, their criticism is more likely to be productive. I knew that this particular reviewer really loved jazz and had devoted a good portion of his life to studying it. He cared for jazz in the best way he knew how—by reviewing artists. He was not gentle, but he was direct, and I did my best to push aside his harsh delivery for the truth of its content. Then I prayed for direction as to how I might apply this truth to my life.

It was painful and difficult. I felt like something inside me was dying, and in a way, that was true—submitting to the truth of life is like dying sometimes. Something dies within us when we meditate on the sorrowful mysteries too.

The meditations of the rosary are a direct and lifelong answer to our desire to accept the truth about ourselves, to become willing to shed that which isn't working, to progress in intimacy, and to become more like God. The prayer "God, show me how to inhabit myself, to be more like you" continues to lead me to the sorrowful mysteries, a portrayal in graphic detail of our unwillingness to embrace divine direction, of the consequences of our sin, and of the beauty of restraint and silence.

You may be asking, "Why in the world would anyone in their right mind want to purposely meditate on events as grotesque and terrible as sweating blood, scourging at a pillar, and crucifixion?" Scripture urges us to think on that which is lovely (Philippians 4:8). How could anyone ever come to see the sorrowful mysteries as lovely? But while I was conducting interviews for this book, I heard the same sentiment over and over: "I hated the sorrowful mysteries at first, but now they're my favorite." Or, "I always felt uncomfortable meditating on the sorrowful mysteries, but now I pray them every day."

The truth is that the passion of Christ was the highest form of love. Such love cannot be anything but lovely. It was a gradual process, but eventually I came to understand that the sorrowful mysteries are nestled among the joyful, the luminous, and the glorious for a reason. Without the mix of joy and light followed by sorrow, there was no way to get to glory. The ordering of the rosary mirrors the balance that God has given the universe: one part joy, one part light, one part sorrow, one part glory. All equal, all essential, all a very natural part of the process.

I think that too often our cultural tendency is to never acknowledge true pain and suffering. We waltz through painful experience after painful experience telling ourselves, "That didn't hurt!" Meanwhile, we are stockpiling a whole mountain of hurts. But it might be wise, as writer Julia Cameron suggests, to say instead, "That did hurt, but I will heal." Christ gives us the ideal example of this during the agony in the garden, when he prays for relief from imminent pain and is willing to acknowledge it as such. Pain is a natural part of life, a necessary messenger. Sacrifice, though painful, is essential for spiritual growth. Pain lets us know that a problem indeed exists. The message of the sorrowful mysteries is that because of our sin, we're in need of a Savior. The good news of the sorrowful mysteries is that one indeed exists.

Christ is the essential figure in suffering. With him, suffering has redemptive value. Without him, suffering is futile.

In his autobiography, Thomas Merton writes about the death of his father when Merton was still a teenager and not a Christian:

> We were in the condition of most of the world, the condition of men without faith in the presence of war, disease, pain, starvation, suffering, plague, bombardment, death. You just had to take it, like a dumb animal. Try to avoid it, if you could. But you must eventually reach the point where you can't avoid it any more. Take it. Try to stupefy yourself, if you like, so that it won't hurt so much. But you will always have to take some of it. And it will all devour you in the end.

Indeed, the truth that many people never understand until it is too late is that the more you try to avoid suffering, the more you suffer, because smaller and more insignificant things begin to torture you in proportion to your fear of being hurt. The one who does most to avoid suffering is, in the end, the one who suffers most: and his suffering comes to him from things so little and so trivial that one can say that it is no longer objective at all. It is his own existence, his own being, that is at once the subject and the source of his pain, and his very existence and consciousness is his greatest torture. This is another of the great perversions by which the devil uses our philosophies to turn our whole nature inside out, and eviscerate all our capacities for good, turning them against ourselves.

We want to shrink back from suffering, but that very action would be the cause of our demise. We want to entirely remove the cross from the equation of life. Although we wish the order of things were different, the fact remains that suffering has purpose, that it is indeed an essential part of the plan. And, as reflected in the rosary, suffering is neither the beginning nor the end of the plan, but is certainly in the mix.

Mary's presence in the sorrowful mysteries deepens their meaning. To watch another in pain is a different kind of suffering. Especially if you are witnessing the suffering of someone close to you, someone with whom you would trade places in a moment if it would end their agony, someone whose suffering you would be willing to take on yourself for love of them. That was Mary's position as she watched her Son suffer and die.

In collecting interviews for this book, I found many parents who prayed the sorrowful mysteries for their children. As parents, they marveled at Mary's own fortitude to watch her most precious and only Son, the flesh of her flesh, go through such torture. They wondered how any parent could withstand it. And so it drew them closer to the heart of the Blessed Mother.

One young man, soon to be a father, would often pray the rosary with his wife each night as they lay in bed together.

"You understand more of Mary's sorrow, watching her have to suffer as she watched her Son," he said. "I could look at my wife and understand how much she loved our unborn child even before he was born and think, this is what Mary went through. It wasn't just abstract to me anymore. It makes me understand Christ more, not just as man, but as God. Praying it in the context of parenthood, I realize that we're going to have a lot of suffering with our child. . . . No parent doesn't have suffering. I like to think that the sorrowful mysteries are preparing me for that. The joy of parenting is also going to come with suffering. . . . But that's all a part of God's plan too."

What are your crosses to bear? What are the sufferings of your heart, mind, or body? Are you unsatisfied with your work, at odds with a neighbor, annoyed by your spouse? Do you perhaps suffer from a chronic illness, overwhelming grief at the death of a loved one, loneliness, or an addictive compulsion? Bring them all to the sorrowful mysteries in meditation and see how Christ might transform them into that which is lovely.

The First Sorrowful Mystery: The Agony in the Garden

Then Jesus went with them to a place called Gethsemane; and he said to his disciples, "Sit here while I go over there and pray." He took with him Peter and the two sons of Zebedee, and began to be grieved and agitated. Then he said to them, "I am deeply grieved, even to death; remain here, and stay awake with me." And going a little farther, he threw himself on the ground and prayed, "My Father, if it is possible, let this cup pass from me; yet not what I want but what you want." Then he came to the disciples and found them sleeping; and he said to Peter, "So, could you not stay awake with me one hour? Stay awake and pray that you may not come into the time of trial; the spirit indeed is willing, but the flesh is weak." Again he went away for the second time and prayed, "My Father, if this cannot pass unless I drink it, your will be done." Again he came and found them sleeping, for their eyes were heavy. So leaving them again, he went away and prayed for the third time, saying the same words. Then he came to the disciples and said to them, "Are you still sleeping and taking your rest? See, the hour is at hand, and the Son of Man is betrayed into the hands of sinners." (Matthew 26:36–45)

When faced with the reality of the impending Crucifixion, the Messiah falls to his knees in prayer. Jesus experienced anguish as any human being in the same circumstances would. And yet he was able to say, "not my will, but yours be done." He did not act on his feelings, but simply honored them and then offered them back to God in trust. *Not my way, but yours.* This is a moment not just of complete submission to the will of the Father but of acute emotional integrity.

> *Lord, so often when I suffer emotional anguish I either work myself into a panic or I try to deny my feelings altogether. I will be stoic, I will live in denial, I will resist your gentle prompting—all of which draw me away from your will. But your example, Jesus, lets me know that having painful feelings is sometimes a part of the plan. That doesn't mean I have to act on them. I can be honest about what I feel without letting those feelings immaturely dictate my behavior.*
>
> *Help me accept my suffering as you accepted yours. Help me be honest with you about my fear and not deny it like a fool, only to act on it anyway. Then I can offer up my feelings, just like Jesus, with this prayer: "Not what I want, but what you want." Help me trust that your will is always to draw me nearer to you, even when it feels like you're far away. Remind me that it is always safe for me to bring myself to you, just as I am, even if I'm fearful, angry, emotional, or in agony.*

I pray for emotional integrity and for the trust and vulnerability I need to follow you, even when the way looks too rough to pass.

The Second Sorrowful Mystery: The Scourging at the Pillar

Now at the festival the governor was accustomed to release a prisoner for the crowd, anyone whom they wanted. At that time they had a notorious prisoner, called Jesus Barabbas. So after they had gathered, Pilate said to them, "Whom do you want me to release for you, Jesus Barabbas or Jesus who is called the Messiah?" For he realized that it was out of jealousy that they had handed him over. While he was sitting on the judgment seat, his wife sent word to him, "Have nothing to do with that innocent man, for today I have suffered a great deal because of a dream about him." Now the chief priests and the elders persuaded the crowds to ask for Barabbas and to have Jesus killed. The governor again said to them, "Which of the two do you want me to release for you?" And they said, "Barabbas." Pilate said to them, "Then what should I do with Jesus who is called the Messiah?" All of them said, "Let him be crucified!" Then he asked, "Why, what evil has he done?" But they shouted all the more, "Let him be crucified!"

So when Pilate saw that he could do nothing, but rather that a riot was beginning, he took some water and washed his hands before the crowd, saying, "I am innocent of this man's blood; see to it yourselves." Then the people as a whole answered, "His blood

*be on us and on our children!" So he released Barabbas for them;
and after flogging Jesus, he handed him over to be crucified.
(Matthew 27:15–26)*

When Pilate could find no fault in Jesus, he cowered before
the crowd. As if crucifixion was not enough, Pilate also flogged
Jesus, just for good measure. How useless! Such a waste! All sin
is pointless, leading to nothing productive, nothing that even
makes sense. The scourging of Jesus is a potent example of the
futility of all sin. And the fury of it.

How quickly our hate is stirred within us, how quickly our
hate will lead us to places where reason can no longer reach us,
where compassion is ushered out at the crack of a whip against
bare flesh. How quickly the chasm of hate can fill up, bringing
us to our most savage selves, torturing and killing just because
we can.

*Lord, I do not want to be a part of the angry crowd. I do not
want to give in to the pressures around me, but I am easily
swayed to places beyond reason. Help me when I feel that I
am surrounded on all sides by senseless acts of cruelty, violence, or hatred. Help me to see sense, reason, and, above
all, compassion. Give me the courage to do what is right,
even if it means standing alone, like Jesus that day, bearing
hateful, undeserved, flesh-ripping blows.*

I pray for the virtues of justice, fortitude, and compassion.

The Third Sorrowful Mystery: The Crowning with Thorns

Then the soldiers of the governor took Jesus into the governor's head-quarters, and they gathered the whole cohort around him. They stripped him and put a scarlet robe on him, and after twisting some thorns into a crown, they put it on his head. They put a reed in his right hand and knelt before him and mocked him, saying, "Hail, King of the Jews!" They spat on him, and took the reed and struck him on the head. (Matthew 27:27–30)

Stripped, beaten, spit upon, mocked, crowned with thorns. Is this the king?

Some days, circumstances rise up to engulf me. They hiss to me their lies that everything in which I have placed my faith has let me down, has failed me. It seems that there is no way out. The world will try to convince me that I am a fool and that I am not who I think I am, in you.

Lord, help me to remember that I am not defined by my circumstances, no matter how overwhelming or humiliating they feel at times. My value is not dictated by the actions of others toward me, but by your love for me. Remind me that I am always a child of royalty, created by you to be your child, always precious and eternal, no matter what my circumstances may want to suggest. And, like you, I can withstand with dignity those who would choose to mock me and scorn me for your sake. You are king.

I pray for the virtue of a steadfast humility that never forgets my true identity.

The Fourth Sorrowful Mystery: The Carrying of the Cross

After mocking him, they stripped him of the robe and put his own clothes on him. Then they led him away to crucify him.

As they went out, they came upon a man from Cyrene named Simon; they compelled this man to carry his cross. And when they came to a place called Golgotha (which means Place of a Skull), they offered him wine to drink, mixed with gall; but when he tasted it, he would not drink it. (Matthew 27:31–34)

The Passion continues its torturous course when Christ is forced to carry the very thing that will eventually kill him. Splinters of wood and grains of dirt were forced into the open wounds on his ripped back. All the while, the crowds continued to watch and mock and spit and taunt. Simon of Cyrene had to be forced to help Jesus.

Have I been like Simon, only willing to join you in God's work when I am forced to do so? Have I been unwilling to help others around me when they are struggling with their crosses? I have been given crosses too, like everyone. Have I born them disquietly?

Father, give me a deeper understanding of the cross I carry. That we are given trials to strengthen us is a mystery I cannot comprehend. Like your cross, the very thing that threatens me is also the thing that will bring me life. Show me the value of the crosses in my life. Show me how I might join them to yours so that they might have redemptive value. Show me new ways to bear them, new ways to offer them up for your sake. Help me to celebrate and learn from your long suffering, your fortitude, your perseverance.

And when I fear the future, when I'm too afraid or too tired to take another step forward, send me a helper.

I pray for the virtue of perseverance and for a heart that is always willing to help.

The Fifth Sorrowful Mystery: The Crucifixion and Death of Jesus on the Cross

And when they had crucified him, they divided his clothes among themselves by casting lots; then they sat down there and kept watch over him. Over his head they put the charge against him, which read, "This is Jesus, the King of the Jews."

Then two bandits were crucified with him, one on his right and one on his left. Those who passed by derided him, shaking their heads and saying, "You who would destroy the temple and build it in three days, save yourself! If you are the Son of God, come down from the cross." In the same way the chief priests also, along with the scribes and elders, were mocking him, saying, "He saved others; he cannot save himself. He is the King of Israel; let him come down from the cross now, and we will believe in him. He trusts in God; let God deliver him now, if he wants to; for he said, 'I am God's Son.'" The bandits who were crucified with him also taunted him in the same way.

From noon on, darkness came over the whole land until three in the afternoon. And about three o'clock Jesus cried with a loud voice, "Eli, Eli, lema sabachthani?" that is, "My God, my God, why have you forsaken me?" When some of the bystanders heard it, they said, "This man is calling for Elijah." At once one of them ran and got a sponge, filled it with sour wine, put it on a stick, and gave it to him to drink. But the others said, "Wait, let us see whether Elijah will come to save him." Then Jesus cried again with a loud voice and breathed his last. At that moment the curtain of the temple was torn in two, from top to bottom. The earth shook, and the rocks were split. (Matthew 27:35–51)

We see the gruesome details, the nails in the hands and feet, the jeering crowds, the horror of the word *forsaken.* But when we look at the Crucifixion more closely, another truth unfolds. As with a newborn being cradled by his father, it is not in the father's great strength where the child finds security and comfort, but rather in the restraint of the father's strength. There is an equal and opposite reaction to our sin—it is this deep mystery of arms outstretched in agony, arms outstretched in the most humble restraint, arms outstretched in patience, awaiting the gentle, final embrace of heaven. Oh, beloved, even the earth cried out with trembling and darkness.

Father, in what areas of my life are you restraining your strength? In what areas do I need to completely surrender my control and reach out for your loving, nail-scarred hands, even if it's painful?

Lord, please continue to show me that it is not always in your displays of strength and power where I will find my greatest security and comfort, but in your greatest act of submission: this Crucifixion, this death, this mysterious embrace of indescribable love, this sacrifice that makes grace possible. Show me that the answer does not always lie in the removal of pain, that sometimes we are asked instead to throw our arms wide open to accept it. Remind me that such sacrifices are met with trembling, even from within the earth.

I pray for the virtues of patience and self-control.

From Prison to Premed

Charles is a young, handsome college student. Just twenty-five years old, he combines an inoffensive youthful bravado with a lovely mix of humility and delight. His smile is brilliant enough to knock you down. And Charles has many reasons to smile these days.

We spoke one Saturday afternoon while sitting on the steps outside a local church where he was anticipating going to confession. Despite attending school full-time and working almost full-time, he still manages to go as often as twice a week.

"I don't want *anything* keeping me from heaven!" he said, smiling. "Even if it's little."

His ardor for keeping his side of the street clean did not come easily. In fact, it came at quite a price. Although he was raised in a devoutly Catholic family by parents who attended daily Mass and often prayed the rosary with their children, Charles abandoned his faith when he was a teenager. It wasn't long before circumstances separated him from his parents and he was out on his own, living with another family member. He was just fifteen. Without the watchful guidance of his parents, he was soon drawn into the wrong crowd, doing poorly in school, getting into fistfights, and worse.

"I was deviating from the way I was brought up," he said. "My parents were very devout."

Loneliness and fear kept Charles headed down the wrong road. His friends got involved with drugs, and it wasn't long before Charles had to pay the price for tempting disaster.

"I knew what I was getting into," he said. "It's not an excuse coming from where I came from. When I was in school, I was picked on and I felt bad and I wanted to make friends, and in order to look important, I needed to be around the popular guys. It seems like the more bad you did, the more trouble you got into, the more popular you were! So I got into trouble, but it was a fortunate thing for me because it helped me to change my life and to get back to God."

"Trouble" for Charles came in the form of prison. One day while driving down the highway, he and his friends were pulled over and arrested for drug possession. Charles received a two-year sentence.

"I knew I had to get back to doing the right thing," he said. "Praying the rosary was the easiest way for me to get back to what I knew. It was what I grew up on. When I started praying the rosary, it was easier for me to change my ways."

Prison was a sobering and frightening experience for Charles, who was nineteen at the time. He said he was most frightened by what other prisoners with life sentences and nothing to lose might do to stir up trouble for a first-time offender with a relatively short sentence.

"They weren't getting out no matter what," he said, "so what did it matter if they beat someone up or whatever? They could cause trouble and they didn't care. The condition in prison is not a good condition. . . . People come in there with six-month sentences and end up doing life sentences. . . . I prayed the rosary a lot of times and tried to read my Bible."

While still in prison and feeling dejected, hopeless, and unsure, he asked Mary for a sign that she was indeed hearing his prayers, that he was not alone. One evening, after the lights had been turned out, his rosary started glowing in the dark. His rosary has glowed on many occasions, even since he was released from prison. At times, Charles has also received a very strong, sweet smell while praying the rosary.

"I was baffled!" he said, shaking his head and turning his gaze to the ground in bashful humility.

The sorrowful mysteries soon became his favorite, and he still tries to pray the sorrowful mysteries in addition to whatever mysteries are generally suggested for the day.

"When I meditate on them, I realize how much Christ suffered, as well as the Blessed Mother," said Charles, "and I try to imagine what he was going through. When I meditate on the agony in the garden, I keep thinking about when I was waiting to be assigned to a prison. . . . I didn't know what prison would be like. I was agonizing, 'Maybe they will kill me.' . . . Until I went there I didn't know.

"It makes me sad that more people don't take advantage of the rosary," he added. "It's there to help us. The rosary is so good, anyone who doesn't have a strong faith, that's what the rosary is there for really—having that faith."

After he completed his prison sentence, Charles did indeed turn his life around, something he attributes to God, the Blessed Mother, and praying the rosary. He worked full-time for several years before returning to school, where he is currently majoring in premed.

"I want to give something back," he said. "People do rehabilitate. This is the life of God coming out in me. The grace of God changed me. Now I'm in school and doing excellent, and it's the miracle of God. I give all the praises to God."

The Promise of Glory:
The Glorious Mysteries

*To them God chose to make known how great . . . are
the riches of the glory of this mystery, which is Christ in
you, the hope of glory.*
—Colossians 1:27

The sorrowful mysteries acknowledge the pain and suffering of
life. The glorious mysteries answer that pain with unshakable
conviction: "But through God's grace, I will heal." But how so?
What is glory?

Noted Christian apologist C. S. Lewis answers this question
brilliantly in "The Weight of Glory." Lewis writes, "Either glory
means to me fame, or it means luminosity." He goes on to suggest that fame, by its nature of making a person more well-
known than others, must certainly be "a competitive passion
and therefore of hell rather than heaven. As for the second, who
wishes to become a kind of living electric light bulb?" Neither of
these, says Lewis, is an accurate description of God's glory, but
to me, the lightbulb idea is somewhat appealing. I imagine that

events like Pentecost and Paul's conversion were filled with strong, immediate light, like the kind that appears when you turn on a lightbulb in a pitch-black room.

Lewis is right about the problems of the glory of worldly fame. I've tasted the tiniest amount of this. I've been written about in newspapers and have had the occasional experience of driving down the road and hearing myself singing on the car radio. On very rare occasions, I have been stopped in city streets by someone who wanted my autograph. My voice has even inspired a few to fall madly in love with me—most recently, the eight-year-old son of the nurse who gives me my allergy shots.

While these events are fun, they are not events that light one up from the inside. They only light one up from the outside—and often fleetingly—and sometimes have grim effects. It is easy to submit to arrogance or people pleasing or to get trapped in the cycle of "never enough." Fame brings a craving for more fame—more adulation, bigger audiences, more awards, higher sales figures, more publicity. A ravenous need claws from the inside, trying desperately to obtain the sustenance it requires from the outside. But satisfying it is always a futile attempt, because the more you feed it, the hungrier and nastier it becomes. I've seen firsthand what serious fame can do to those in the spotlight.

I've also had just a taste, a tiny glimpse, of the "lightbulb" type of glory. I've sometimes felt it at Mass, in eucharistic adoration and in the sacraments, and often when I sing. I've felt it when I've been in the presence of others who live in search of heavenly glory and thereby share in it to some degree while still on earth. To possess this kind of glory means that you are infused, through no effort or merit of your own, with a light so brilliant and so perfectly heated that you can find your way without stumbling and can warm yourself by it without getting burned.

Glory requires a difficult balance. Scripture is full of warnings about it. "May I never boast of anything except the cross of our Lord Jesus Christ" (Galatians 6:14), said St. Paul. Glory has nothing to do with us and everything to do with God and God in us. It is a problem of recognition, of identification—both of ourselves and of God. True glory isn't something we can obtain on our own. In that way, it somewhat resembles mere fame; we depend on something outside of ourselves in order to obtain it. But the difference between true glory and fame is God. He is working in us, and it is his desire to bring us into eternal glory. With earthly celebrity, other people inhabit that place within us; they determine our worth, our value, our worthiness to be loved. True glory is about God determining our worthiness to be loved.

The goal of glory is becoming a "good and faithful servant," pleasing in the eyes of God. We want to earn God's approval, God's blessing. "For glory means good report with God, acceptance by God, response, acknowledgment, and welcome into the heart of things," said Lewis. In the dissonance of our culture, it is all too easy to lose sight of what the real goal is. That's not to say that life should not be enjoyed. On the contrary, the glory of God is the very thing that gives life its tremendous value.

The glorious mysteries challenge us with difficult questions: When did we become so complacent, so satisfied with so little? When did we become so willing to fall short of the mark? What has eroded our desire for heaven? What has covered up that intrinsic ache to be with God? The messages of our culture win out. We've grown ignorant. We raise our children to aspire to fame and fortune rather than to the fulfillment of God's call. As Lewis said, we have become like a small child who is satisfied to play in the mud in a slum because, despite the offer, he cannot imagine building a sand castle at the seashore.

We need to remember who we are and who God is and why it is that we hope in him. Alas, our hope brings pain. We hope for the thing that has not yet come. As St. Paul said, we "groan inwardly while we wait for adoption, the redemption of our bodies" (Romans 8:23). We don't like to admit our aches, and we don't like to feel them, so we medicate them. But there is no painkiller for this ache. The only solution is, as Lewis says, "to be at last summoned inside, [which] would be both glory and honor beyond all our merits and also the healing of that old ache." That ache to be with God, which nothing of this earth can ever fill, becomes a source of direction and life. Pentecost was as much a filling with that glowing ache, or "glory ache," as it was a filling with the Holy Spirit. The Holy Spirit, by his nature, always wants to return to his triune home. We are full, yet still aching. Aching to go home.

Of all the human beings to ever walk this earth, surely Mary must have experienced that ache most acutely. Joined with her Savior in their unique relationship, she must have glowed in the most intense yet inconspicuous way, as if a kind of quiet fire burned within her, as if a kind of private luminosity directed her steps and attracted others to her. She knew her glory came from the Lord. "My soul magnifies the Lord," she said, "my spirit rejoices in God my Savior, for he has looked with favor on the lowliness of his servant" (Luke 1:46–48). Her body was redeemed because she ached perfectly, and therefore she celebrated in God's glory perfectly.

God has not created us with a longing that he does not intend to satisfy at some point. St. Paul reminds us that "those whom he predestined he also called; and those whom he called he also justified; and those whom he justified he also glorified" (Romans 8:30). The glorious mysteries are God's commitment to satisfying that longing within us. They are the official announcement that it is okay to hope, that, in fact, he demands it of us and has created us for it.

What do you hope for? A better job, a college education, to fall in love? Do you hope for healing or for wisdom or for things to simply work out? Where do you go with your hope? Where does your interior gaze fall? Does it seem too risky, too frightening, too ridiculous to raise it toward heaven? Do you long to burn with something greater and brighter, a light that is perfectly warm and pure and pleasing to you and to God? He longs to arrest and give purpose to our aches, even those we are afraid to show people, even those we may be reluctant to admit to ourselves.

Go ahead, hope for glory. You were designed to.

The First Glorious Mystery: The Resurrection

After the sabbath, as the first day of the week was dawning, Mary Magdalene and the other Mary went to see the tomb. And suddenly there was a great earthquake; for an angel of the Lord, descending from heaven, came and rolled back the stone and sat on it. His appearance was like lightning, and his clothing white as snow. For fear of him the guards shook and became like dead men. But the angel said to the women, "Do not be afraid; I know that you are looking for Jesus who was crucified. He is not here; for he has been raised, as he said. Come, see the place where he lay. Then go quickly and tell his disciples, 'He has been raised from the dead, and indeed he is going ahead of you to Galilee; there you will see him.' This is my message for you." So they left the tomb quickly with fear and great joy, and ran to tell his disciples. Suddenly Jesus met them and said, "Greetings!" And they came to him, took hold of his feet, and worshiped him. Then Jesus said to them, "Do not be afraid; go and tell my brothers to go to Galilee; there they will see me." (Matthew 28:1–10)

"They will see me," the resurrected Christ says. "They will see me." What a promise! If hopelessness is the inability to see something better, the Resurrection is the epitome of hope. Here, the most hopeless of circumstances has been entirely reversed.

Because something is beyond my comprehension does not make it untrue. This mystery reminds me that the ways of God will often be beyond my comprehension. I want to live with an attitude that believes: *They will see me.*

In the promise of the Resurrection, I am not left to myself: Christ has transformed my arrogance into confidence, my greed into generosity, my lusts into chastity and temperance, my pride into humility, my self-pity into gratitude, and my resentment into forgiveness and freedom. In the weight of that promise, I can live in hope and share someday in glory. That promise is for me too.

O Lord, you have met us with an impossible, unexpected love, a love so strong it drew life from the grave. Give me the ability to see it! Give me your vision of hope—hope in you and in your promises, for this life and the next. Grant me the ability to see the best possible outcome, the ability to trust in your unexpected ways, and the grace to accept them, for I want to see you too.

I pray for the virtue of a thriving hope.

The Second Glorious Mystery: The Ascension

So when they had come together, they asked him, "Lord, is this the time when you will restore the kingdom to Israel?" He replied, "It is not for you to know the times or periods that the Father has set by his own authority. But you will receive power when the Holy Spirit has come upon you; and you will be my witnesses in Jerusalem, in all Judea and Samaria, and to the ends of the earth." When he had said this, as they were watching, he was lifted up, and a cloud took him out of their sight. While he was going and they were gazing up toward heaven, suddenly two men in white robes stood by them. They said, "Men of Galilee, why do you stand looking up toward heaven? This Jesus, who has been taken up from you into heaven, will come in the same way as you saw him go into heaven." (Acts 1:6–11)

He was lifted up. The direction of Christ's movement gives us some idea of where we may turn when we are in need of inspiration. It was from heaven that the Holy Spirit descended on Mary, and it was to heaven that Christ ascended. On this path to and from heaven is where we want to walk. When we meditate, we can practice a small act of ascension in our thoughts and prayers, through the presence and intercession of the Holy Spirit.

> *Lord, in the same way you ascended into heaven, body and soul, I want to keep my thoughts and my interior gaze always directed heavenward—looking to heaven for help when I have grown weary, looking to heaven for inspiration, so that I might always aspire to be worthy of heaven. Keep my eyes on heaven and on the promise of eternal life, not on the obstacles and sin that sometimes seem to surround me. Show me, Lord, where I might find evidence of heaven here, in the people I love, in the sacraments, in the beauty of this earth, in the miracle of life, and in the loveliness and frailty*

of humanity. Give me the same kind of levity of spirit that you gave so many of the saints, allowing them to see the beauty of heaven in even the smallest, most insignificant things: a bird, a flower, a fallen leaf.

Father, I pray for a greater levity of spirit and for a greater desire to rise above my circumstances and sin to reach for the Savior.

The Third Glorious Mystery: The Descent of the Holy Spirit upon the Apostles at Pentecost

When the day of Pentecost had come, they were all together in one place. And suddenly from heaven there came a sound like the rush of a violent wind, and it filled the entire house where they were sitting. Divided tongues, as of fire, appeared among them, and a tongue rested on each of them. All of them were filled with the Holy Spirit and began to speak in other languages, as the Spirit gave them ability. (Acts 2:1–4)

The same Holy Spirit that overshadowed Mary at the Annunciation now visits the apostles at Pentecost. He descends upon them to *give them ability*—to speak, to heal, to exhort, to edify. This is the same Holy Spirit that is available to us now.

Lord, how often I burn only with my own desires, and how quickly such flames burn out, leaving me cold and in the dark. But your fire in me is eternal. It cannot be quickly snuffed out by the least little breeze. It cannot be washed out with a few drops of rain. It cannot be stamped out by aimless pursuits, excess, or fear.

As I pray this mystery, I ask that you send forth your Holy Spirit and the gifts that accompany that burning passion—discernment, wisdom, exhortation, moral courage, healing, and deep conversion. Fan this eternal flame each day so that I burn ever more brightly, desiring only your will for me and to serve your purposes. This, I know, will bring me the greatest satisfaction and peace.

Father, come and fill me with your divine breath.

The Fourth Glorious Mystery: The Assumption

Arise, shine; for your light has come, and the glory of the LORD has risen upon you. For darkness shall cover the earth, and thick darkness the peoples; but the LORD will arise upon you, and his glory will appear over you. Nations shall come to your light, and kings to the brightness of your dawn. (Isaiah 60:1–3)

Mary's purity brought about the redemption of her body. Like her Son, she was taken up to heaven. Unlike her Son, she was taken up not through her own power, but through God's power due to her complete cooperation with his plan.

Dear Blessed Mother, yours was a glory that came from your deep longing for Christ. You hoped for him as the Messiah, you nurtured him as your Son, you ached with him during his passion and death, and you hoped in him once again upon his resurrection and ascension. The glory that lived in you burned away all impurity and prepared you for the Assumption. I pray that from your example I might also learn to glory in the Lord and in the great things he has done for me. May he also fill me with the graces appropriate to my calling.

I pray for the virtue of purity

The Fifth Glorious Mystery: The Coronation

Then God's temple in heaven was opened, and the ark of his covenant was seen within his temple; and there were flashes of lightning, rumblings, peals of thunder, an earthquake, and heavy hail.

A great portent appeared in heaven: a woman clothed with the sun, with the moon under her feet, and on her head a crown of twelve stars. (Revelation 11:19–12:1)

The queen is coming! We must prepare. We must sew splendid garments and serve elegant feasts. We must bring out the very best silver and the most exquisite china. We must decorate with flowers and jewels and celebrate with music and dancing. The queen, this most faithful servant, is coming! She has come to be near her child. And what a heavenly homecoming awaits her.

Heaven is preparing a homecoming for us too.

Mary, Queen of Heaven, your castle is your purity, your kingdom is your virtue, and your crowning jewel is your complete cooperation in God's plan of salvation. Mary, Queen of Peace, pray for us.

I pray for the virtue of piety.

Marriage Reborn

I met Beverly and Chuck, a married couple in their sixties, at a rosary walk, where devotees gather to pray together for deceased family members. It began in a cemetery in Nashville. Beverly and Chuck were beginning a novena for their parents. Part of the devotion involved visiting a cemetery every day during the novena to remember the dead.

"We thought this would be a good way to start," said Beverly. The couple says the complete rosary every day, all fifteen decades. Their rosary devotion has grown particularly strong over the past few years. Chuck claimed that since he started saying the rosary, "everything is different. My life is totally changed, everything is much better, peaceful."

Beverly added, "You just learn to trust, to trust in the Lord."

Their story certainly tested the boundaries of trust. After thirty-two years of marriage, Beverly and Chuck divorced. Six years later, they reconciled and have been remarried for two years. Both possess an obvious delight; though soft-spoken and somewhat shy, they were happy to talk about their experience with rosary devotion. Both attributed their surprising reconciliation to the rosary.

"Of course, we never thought that would happen," said Beverly. "Our kids never thought that would happen, and it was through the Blessed Lady that we got back together."

Chuck added, "It was a somewhat bitter divorce and it affected all the kids, and so when we got back together it was quite a shock to them and it happened quite quickly too. The rosary is very, very powerful. As you say the rosary, you receive graces that give you strength."

Beverly agreed: "The fact is, our marriage is a lot better now."

Chuck was equally enthusiastic. "I can't say enough about the rosary, it's such a powerful prayer. It's the second most powerful prayer after the Mass. . . . It's a powerful weapon."

A Place to Grow:
Variations on the Rosary

The rosary is really a training program for deeper prayer.
—Francesco, college student

A multitude of variations on the rosary have sprung up since it was first developed, particularly over the last century. All offer deeper communion with God through meditation on more specific areas of his divinity. For example, the Rosary to the Holy Wounds meditates on Christ's wounds on the cross. Many variations have developed as a result of the private revelations of particularly devout individuals. The Chaplet of Divine Mercy, associated with the revelations given to St. Faustina Kowalska, is perhaps the most popular of these.

All variations are optional. Many people have found them to be effective ways to deepen prayer, and I encourage you to look into them if you are so led. Two examples follow.

The Rosary to the Holy Wounds

The Rosary to the Holy Wounds was derived from the writings of Blessed Sr. Mary Martha Chambon (1841–1907) of the Monastery of the Visitation of Chambery. Her writings involve meditation on the wounds of Christ on the cross. This devotion may be especially helpful to anyone who is suffering a wound, be it physical, emotional, or spiritual. The devotion calls for the following prayers:

On the crucifix, pray:
O Jesus, divine redeemer, be merciful to us and to the whole world. Amen.

On the next three beads, pray:
Strong God, holy God, immortal God, have mercy on us and on the whole world. Amen.

Grace and mercy, O my Jesus, during present dangers; cover us with your precious blood. Amen.

Eternal Father, grant us mercy through the blood of Jesus Christ, your only Son; grant us mercy, we beseech you. Amen. Amen. Amen.

On the large beads, pray the following. If you are praying in a communal setting, one person (the leader) will read the first prayer, and the rest will respond with the second prayer. If you are praying by yourself, pray both prayers.

V. Eternal Father, I offer you the wounds of our Lord, Jesus Christ.
R. To heal the wounds of our souls.

On the small beads, pray:
V. My Jesus, pardon and mercy.
R. Through the merits of your holy wounds.

The writings of Blessed Sr. Chambon promise conversion and mercy for those who pray this prayer. In her private revelation, Jesus says:

> You must put your soul and those of your companions into My sacred Wounds; there they will become perfected as gold in the furnace. . . . Plunge your actions into My Wounds and they will be of value. . . . My Wounds will repair yours. . . . When you have some trouble, something to suffer, quickly place it in My Wounds, and the pain will be alleviated quickly.

Christ's wounds can repair ours. As St. Paul says, when we suffer and offer that suffering to the cause of Christ, our suffering becomes not only bearable but also useful (Romans 8:17). Christ's suffering also gives us an appropriate context for our own pain. Christ's wounds can change the nature of our wounds, from that which strips us of life to that which gives life and is life sustaining.

The Chaplet of Divine Mercy

The Chaplet of Divine Mercy is a rosary tradition derived from the Divine Mercy devotion associated with St. Faustina Kowalska, a Polish nun who died in the 1930s. St. Faustina, who was canonized by Pope John Paul II in 2000, received many visions and private revelations testifying to God's boundless mercy for suffering humanity. This Divine Mercy devotion is an especially welcome message for our age. Millions of people around the world say the Chaplet of Divine Mercy daily. Many say it daily at 3:00 p.m., which is, according to St. Faustina, the hour of divine mercy.

The Chaplet of Divine Mercy consists of the following prayers. The opening prayer, said before the rosary begins, is taken from St. Faustina's diaries:

> You expired, Jesus, but the source of life gushed forth for souls, and an ocean of mercy opened up for the whole world. O Fount of Life, unfathomable Divine Mercy, envelop the whole world and empty Yourself out upon us. O Blood and Water, which gushed forth from the Heart of Jesus as a fount of mercy for us, I trust in You!

The Our Father, the Hail Mary, and the Apostles' Creed are said as usual. Then the following prayer is said on the large bead before each decade:

Eternal Father, I offer you the body and blood, soul and divinity of your dearly beloved Son, our Lord, Jesus Christ, in atonement for our sins and those of the whole world.

The following prayer is said in addition to the Hail Mary on the ten small beads of each decade:
For the sake of his sorrowful passion, have mercy on us and on the whole world.

The rosary concludes with this prayer:
Holy God, holy mighty one, holy immortal one, have mercy on us and on the whole world.

This closing prayer is optional:
Eternal God, in whom mercy is endless and the treasure of compassion inexhaustible, look kindly upon us and increase your mercy in us, that in difficult moments we might not despair nor become despondent, but with great confidence submit ourselves to your holy will, which is love and mercy itself.

Other Rosary Traditions

Many rich and lovely traditions have developed alongside the two mentioned above. Groups gather around the world in grottoes and hospitals, dorm rooms and living rooms, chapels and fields, parks and cemeteries to recite the rosary together. Sometimes they recite the rosary for special intentions or for thanksgiving for prayers answered, other times to facilitate spiritual preparation, and still other times out of a desire for communal worship.

When I lived in Alaska, I would join the cloistered Sisters of Perpetual Adoration while they prayed their communal rosary every day at 3:00 p.m.. At 6:45 p.m. daily on the campus of the University of Notre Dame, a group assembles to pray the rosary at the grotto of Our Lady, come rain, snow, sleet, or shine. The elementary-school boys of Mater Dei School in Potomac, Maryland, make rosaries as a class on the Feast of Our Lady of the Holy Rosary, October 7. Gene Mulloy and his friends at the Tennessee Center for Peace have made thousands of rosaries for entire elementary schools, high schools, and universities—in their school colors, no less. Many people belong to Perpetual Rosary groups, in which each member is assigned one decade. Each member prays his or her assigned mystery each day, thereby completing an entire rosary in a "mystical communal" experience.

Perhaps the most well-known and practiced of all the rosary traditions are rosary novenas. Novenas have a long history in the church. They are specified times set aside for prayers of reparation, preparation, or intercession. Most novenas last nine days or have some association with the number nine. The reason for the special significance of the number nine is not entirely clear. Some historians say that the number nine honors the nine months that Christ was in Mary's womb. Others say that it marks the nine days between Christ's ascension and Pentecost, during which time the disciples prepared for the coming of the Holy Spirit. Another possibility has to do with the ancient belief that ten is the perfect number, and therefore representative of God. Nine, one short of ten, represents humanity.

Not all novenas last nine days. Some last thirty-three days in celebration of the number of years of Christ's life on earth; others last forty days in remembrance of Christ's forty-day fast in the desert or the forty days he walked the earth following his resurrection. The numbers themselves have no special meaning. A well-prayed novena depends on the condition of the heart of the petitioner, not the petitioner's precision.

Some people express their intentions by beginning or ending novenas on particular days of interest or meaning for them, such as a feast day. Many celebrate rosary novenas during the month of October, a month of honoring Mary, and especially choose to begin on October 7—the Feast of Our Lady of the Holy Rosary. Many people pray novenas in combination with performing a physical action, such as visiting a chapel or attending Mass every day during the novena. Others begin or end novenas on a birthday, a holiday, or the feast day of their patron saint.

Rosary novenas exist to help increase our faith and devotion, and in this way they become an even more powerful expression of devotion. Rosary novenas allow us to have increased and regular communication with God about specific matters of importance to us, and thus serve as powerful opportunities for God to work in our lives.

A Novena for a Wife

Rod, a successful writer in his thirties, was raised as a Methodist but became a Catholic not long after graduating from college. As Rod's faith grew, so did his desire for marriage and family life. He struggled with loneliness and the difficulty of trying to find a suitable lifelong companion.

One day Rod and a neighbor were talking about how difficult it was to meet people. She told Rod a story about an older Italian woman in her office. Numerous single women in her office also wanted to get married, and this woman told them, "Girls, let me tell you what happened to me. . . ." Rod remembers:

"She told this story about how someone had given her a very old and long novena that you prayed for fifty-four days to Our Lady of Pompeii. You pray it for whatever your intention is. She prayed it to find a husband. Sure enough, during the novena cycle, she met a man and fell madly in love with him. On the last day of the novena, he proposed marriage. And they got married and had a brilliant marriage and lots of kids and all of that.

"Now this lady gave the novena to all the women in the office [all Catholics]. Well, every one of the women who prayed that novena got married. . . . And I said, 'Give me that novena! I've got to pray it!'"

This fifty-four-day novena is also called the Irresistible Novena. It began with a private revelation to a girl in Naples. Our Lady of Pompeii appeared to her and told her that she would not refuse any intercession prayed for fifty-four days. The fifty-four-day rosary novena is simply one rosary per day for fifty-four days. Three nine-day novenas are prayed for the intention. Another three nine-day novenas are prayed in thanksgiving, whether or not the petition has been granted at the time. The petitioner meditates on the cycle of the mysteries—joyful, sorrowful, and glorious—one mystery each day until the completion of the novena.

Rod enthusiastically prayed the Irresistible Novena, again and again. But still no wife appeared.

"I can now see that I wasn't nearly ready for marriage," Rod says. "While I was praying for that, God worked some amazing miracles in my life in terms of healing me and making me ready for a wife. I always prayed that if it wasn't God's will that I meet my wife, then God would give me the peace of mind and heart to accept that."

Rod continued to pray. After some time, he prayed the fifty-four-day novena again. Soon after he finished it, he attended a friend's book signing, where he was introduced to a young woman named Julie.

"I was immediately struck by her," he says. "Before the weekend was out we were madly in love with each other. Within a week we were already trading e-mails, saying 'This could be it, you're the one.' Four months later, we were engaged."

Rod says, "When I initially didn't meet a wife, I kept asking myself, 'What's going on?' I could sense that I was changing, but I didn't want to be changed. I wanted to meet a wife! But other things had to happen first. If Julie had walked into my life the day after I finished that first novena, I would not have been ready for her spiritually or emotionally. I kept praying that novena because I had such strong faith in the Blessed Mother. . . . [This novena is] not magic, but it's a matter of faith."

Rod and his wife have prayed the novena for help with many other things as well, including career moves and finding a place to live. They often say the rosary together at night.

_____

Afterword

Padre Pio once said, "The habit of asking 'Why' has ruined the world." It's one of the first things they tell you before you start teaching: "Never phrase your questions to the class as 'why' questions. They are too open-ended and always carry with them a shaming tone." If a student doesn't know the answer to a "why" question, it's somehow more embarrassing than a "how" or "what" or "where" question. I tried to remember that when I was gathering interviews for this book.

Even so, some days it was a difficult task to research a book on the rosary. When I initially approached devotees, many were reserved. In the beginning, I almost wondered if I'd been offensive or inappropriate in some way. Was it my age? My hairstyle? I couldn't understand this overwhelmingly consistent initial reticence.

However, as time wore on, I came to see another pattern, especially with lifelong devotees. Those who had prayed the rosary for any length of time seemed to have developed an unusual piety and humility. To answer a question about their rosary devotion would draw entirely too much attention to them. Once I assured them that my questions were not directed toward them necessarily but more toward the rosary, they were more likely to open up. Once they realized that this was indeed the direction I was interested in pursuing, it was sometimes difficult to get them to *stop* talking, as enthusiastic as they were about the power of this prayer.

Over and over again, I heard how the most hardened of hearts were softened, how the most skeptical became devout, how the most hopeless cases turned around with no other explanation but the intercession of the rosary. Many times people said, "I cannot say enough about the power of the rosary," "It has absolutely changed my life," "I'm not the same person; I am so much more at peace. My life is *real* now."

It occurred to me that perhaps some of the strongest resistance to the rosary comes not from its repetition or from protests regarding Mary's role or even from boredom, but from the simple fact that so few of us truly desire humility, piety, or even peace anymore. I know humility wasn't exactly high on my list when I renewed my practice of praying the rosary. I think we have come to see humility as weakness. I don't long for humility the way the saints longed for humility, the way Mother Teresa wore humility, because I believed the lie that we do not need the virtues, especially humility, anymore.

Pope Pius XI said that the rosary "requires humility of spirit, and, if we disdain humility, as the Divine Redeemer teaches, it will be impossible for us to enter the heavenly kingdom." Christ said, "Truly I tell you, unless you change and become like children, you will never enter the kingdom of heaven" (Matthew 18:3). Sadly, this is a characteristic that our culture seems to avoid at all costs. We want to become like children only in the sense that we want all of our desires met in the moment. For all our talk of the need for tolerance, we are intolerant of taking responsibility. In other words, we act as children without taking on the virtues of children.

To meditate on the life of Christ is to honor and love it. We spend time with that which we love. That which draws our attention has our affection, and how many of us are truly drawn to humility, to sacrifice, to complete surrender? Instead we settle for consumerism and saturate ourselves with meaningless stimuli in order to distract ourselves from the certain pains of life we hope to avoid, wishing the world would change and unable to see that it is we who need to change. It is no wonder we get lost while honoring our intrinsic need to search for love, to hope for glory. Where the world speaks to us of popularity and power, the rosary offers us piety and peace. Rosary devotion has continually challenged me to answer the question "Which will I choose?"

This brings me back to our initial question: "Why the rosary?" I think the answer is because God loves us so dearly and knows us so well. He knows that we need concrete examples of humility, piety, and faith. He knows that these are gifts to be accepted if we will ask for them and that we don't have the capacity to obtain them on our own—they are things we must pray for with passionate patience. But first we must pray just to desire those things. Given the fact that they are virtues after all, why not?

And in our answer, we discover that to which we are truly devoted and, mercifully enough, the one who is entirely devoted to us.

Mary, most devoted, pray for us.